MW00355654

A POET'S JOURNEY THROUGH
LOVE, SUFFERING, & HOPE

THE

MENDED HEART

RHONDA DAWES MILNER

RIVER GROVE
BOOKS

Handwritten inscription:

1/11/19

To Sara,

May you always know God's healing presence in your life.

Love and blessings, Rhonda Dawes Milner

Romans 8:28

Published by River Grove Books
Austin, TX
www.rivergrovebooks.com

Distributed by River Grove Books

Design and composition by Greenleaf Book Group
Cover design by Greenleaf Book Group
Photography by Rhonda Dawes Milner
Mended Heart images by ©Shutterstock.com/Maksim M,
©Shutterstock.com/DeryaDraws

Publisher's Cataloging-in-Publication data is available.

Print ISBN: 978-1-63299-214-7
eBook ISBN: 978-1-63299-216-1

First Edition

To all those whom I have loved and lost, especially my son,
Gene Whitner Milner III. You helped me know feelings and
emotions I would never have known. You helped me connect to
that place deep within, to *The Source*, and that is where poetry
comes from, flowing outward from God. Thank you.

Contents

PREFACE

I BEGAN WRITING POETRY MORE THAN TEN years ago, coinciding with my entry into graduate school. I started by just jotting down phrases or ideas as they came to mind, but then the poem would begin to take on a life of its own. I want to explain this process, starting with a bit of my history.

I was originally a physician, and I am a board-certified radiologist with all my training at Emory University School of Medicine in Atlanta, Georgia. I practiced radiology until I was needed full time at home because of issues with my children. My testimony can be read in full on my website, www.healingpresenceministry.com. I decided after my youngest of four graduated high school that I wanted to do something more interpersonal with people. So, I decided to return to school to work toward a master's degree in professional counseling. The program I selected was integrated with Christian spirituality at Richmont Graduate University. I had two specialties—addiction, along with spirituality and counseling. Simultaneously, I worked toward a certificate in spiritual formation with the Renovaré Institute. Upon completion of these studies in

2013, I decided to pursue a master's degree in ministry and then also became a certified spiritual director, completing training in 2015 at Richmont.

Prior to entering graduate school, I had no formal training in writing and certainly not in poetry. Being a microbiology major in college and a medical student, I never had to write papers, so the voluminous writing required in my graduate studies was a new world for me.

Just prior to my son's death in April 2011, I had completed my first manuscript entitled "Signature of God." I say this because my son was able to read it before his unexpected death. Each chapter began with one of my poems. In the fall of 2015, I asked a good friend whom I highly respected to read my manuscript and offer feedback. He said he thought my manuscript was wonderful and encouraged me to begin sharing my poetry on social media. My first poem shared publicly was "The Divine Paradox," which I posted on on my personal Facebook page. It met with a good reception, so I decided to begin my blog, *Healing Presence Ministry,* which has evolved as primarily a social media–based ministry on Facebook, Instagram, and my website.

Because I am not a trained poet, I view my poetry as a spiritual gift. Writing my poetry is a spiritual experience of a creative nature. It's as if my poems are already written and I act as a mere scribe. They come out in different styles and different lengths when complete. All I normally do is minor editing. I believe when I am especially attuned to God's presence around me and fully present to my deep emotions and feelings, I am able to tap into what I call The Source. This also requires me to be fully open in a super-sensitive state of awareness and receptivity. This may happen at any time of day, including the middle of the night. I often receive poems or inspiration during the night and will wake up to write, fearing they could be lost with daybreak.

My poem "The Source," is about what happens to us when we experience deep emotions, such as love, passion, hurt, or sadness. These emotions can tap into a deep, creative place that lies within us, unleashing it. In our brokenness, we can crack open to discover this silver lining. What is revealed is a powerful connection to the source of all beauty and creativity, our Creator.

Powerful, deep emotions can be provoked by people and incidences that we experience in life. It is not so much about them but what they trigger and release within us. This is where poetry, art, literature, theater, music, dance, and all our creative expressions and experiences originate. It is a channeling of something greater than ourselves. It overflows from within us to others; we are simple vectors or transmitters. It is how great music brings tears to our eyes, how a beautiful painting touches our hearts, or how poetry resonates within our souls. It changes us, moving us spiritually to a better, more enlightened place. In essence, it connects us to others and to God, our life source, The Source.

Beyond time the Source
lives and stands
It remains for us to seek,
to find; it is His plan

The Source

You were the catalyst that helped me discover myself
It wasn't about us, but the ignition of the connection to help me see
A piece was missing that you held and found
No longer will the elusive Source confound
The Source lives deep within a secret place
Untapped, it lies hidden, dormant with no face
It joins us to all humanity and the living
It enables us to know love, receiving and giving
There are different degrees and shades
If not nurtured and fed, it will fade
It sparks and kindles our creative life force
Beauty and art are its main expression, its course
It is how dreams and visions are made
It keeps us bold, fearless, unafraid
Timeless truth, constant it remains
The key to our spiritual growth it contains
To experience connected transcendence
Is the gift, the known consequence
With reflection playing over each and every sign
Otherwise you may miss it, never to find
It allows one to really be present and just be
Harmony with nature, the world, space, it frees
Euphoric bliss, knowing, peace is in the joining; it disarms
The Source is our home; it cannot harm
It is God everywhere, inside, outside in the air
Our deepest connection, why we love and care
Beyond time the Source lives and stands
It remains for us to seek, to find; it is His plan.

God did this so that they would seek him and perhaps reach out for him and find him,
though he is not far from any one of us. "For in him we live and move and have our
being." As some of your own poets have said, "We are his offspring."

ACTS 17:27–28

INTRODUCTION

THE MENDED HEART IS A COLLECTION of poetry and writings about our journey through life as human beings who experience love, suffering, and hope. It is about our spectrum of experiences, both good and bad. It is about joy and happiness, along with pain and sorrow. *Love* and *loss* are both four-letter words that begin with *L*. They are tightly bound. You cannot have one without sooner or later experiencing the other. Like either side of a coin, they exist together.

My poem "On Being Human" expresses and describes this path we all share, and so it introduces the writings I've gathered for you in this book. Despite the varying nationalities, cultures, and faiths we may have—and our different backgrounds and experiences as people—we have the universal feelings of love, suffering, and hope in common. I share with you my experiences in this collection to remind and encourage you that you are never on this journey alone. Life is not easy, and the world can be brutal—even to the innocent—but through love, there always remains hope.

*Being human is connection with
others using our hearts and heads*

*Otherwise we are sentenced to be
the walking living dead*

On Being Human

We are all born as trusting innocents
Then the world of adults steals our resilience

We come with eyes of curiosity and wonder
Then the system breaks our will and thunder

Hearts born so gentle and so tender
Hardened by society they are rendered

But our inner child within still lives
When nurtured and fed, he still can give

Hope, love, virtue, faith, and trust
Come as little children we must

Hardened hearts can then be broken
Through the cracks God's words are spoken

Into our hearts God will live and thrive
But only we can ask Him and decide

Frail humans in elusive, desultory worlds
The enemy is us within tortured and furled

Death breathes close, capturing us all
As we search for significance and meaning
*   before we fall*

Being human is connection with others using
*   our hearts and heads*
Otherwise we are sentenced to be the
*   walking living dead*

All humans need loving, supportive community
It sustains us, offering life and opportunity

It is about relationships finally in the end
Those with God, family, and our friends

Then what will last when we are gone?
It has always been love, our hearts' only song

We come then go as little children once more
As mere humans standing to face death's door.

And now these three remain: faith, hope and love. But the greatest of these is love.

1 CORINTHIANS 13:13

†

In this book, I have grouped the poetry and writings into key parts of our human experience: Love divided into human love (Part One) and God's love (Part Two); then suffering (Part Three); and finally hope (Part Four). What I pray is to bring to my reader encouragement, inspiration, comfort, and hope. I want my words to become a healing presence and a blessing. My ultimate desire is for others to recognize and experience God's love. Then, His love becomes the true healing presence, and I am just the messenger.

PART ONE

Human Love

MATTERS OF THE HEART

MATTERS OF THE HEART AFFECT US to our core, and they also produce effects that determine who we are and who we become.

Matters of the heart are the most important things in our lives that move us deeply. They bring joy and laughter, along with sadness and tears. They are things that touch our hearts, fill our hearts, and break our hearts. They are what make us fully human. Matters of the heart connect us to one another and to God.

*Heart matters cause us to
attach and connect
They give us insight and
make us reflect*

8

Matters of the Heart

What really matters in life?
What protects us from descent and strife?
Things that stir and move our souls
Our true character they shape and mold
Matters of the Heart are sent through prayer
They are about love, compassion, and care
They are when we love strong and deep
They can lead us to cry and make us weep
Heart matters cause us to attach and connect
They give us insight and make us reflect
Emotions and feelings are tightly bound to them
Knowing these hurts with pain can condemn
Heart matters can give us suffering from loss

But we still continue to give our hearts, no
*   matter the cost*
Matters of the Heart make us stop and pause
They are the solutions, not the cause
The heart is our centering main life source
Matters of the Heart are our driving force
Tenderness and sensitivity are worn on the sleeves
They hold us close, not wanting to leave
Matters of the Heart make life worth living
They can deplete us, but they keep us giving

Matters of the Heart draw us to God, never to be alone
Matters of the Heart always help us find our way
*   back home.*

"Above all else, guard your heart, for everything you do flows from it."

PROVERBS 4:23 (NIV)

TO BE LOVED

SOMETIMES IN LIFE, WE MAY FIND a nearly perfect love, someone who loves us close to God's perfect love for us. Often, we receive this from our parents, especially our mothers. But sometimes, we experience this with romantic love.

It is unusual to find unconditional romantic love. There often seem to be so many expectations and requirements to being loved. Rarely, we find this pure love that is just given as a gift with no demands. When we are loved like this, we feel deep connection, complete acceptance, and like we are fully known. We may never experience this kind of human love, but we are always given this perfect love from God, our Father and Creator. My poem "To Be Loved" describes what it is like to receive this kind of love.

Always feeling accepted, never judged
This special love will never
hold anger or a grudge

To Be Loved

What does it mean to be loved and seen?
To be valued for our worth and true being
It is to be fully and wholly known
To always feel we are protected, never alone

To feel secure, resting at peace
Knowing this love will never cease
Feeling lifted up to soar and fly
Knowing we can climb mountains, no matter how high

To never again falter or waver
Knowing we have never felt safer
To feel entirely and totally whole
Never abandoned, never left out in the cold

Feeling feet firmly planted on the ground
Knowing a love like this can never again be found
It makes us strong, giving us strength
Knowing this love cannot be measured by any length

Always feeling accepted, never judged
This special love will never hold
  anger or a grudge
It's our human nature and core need
We need to feel secure, never to leave

To be loved even when we fail
Knowing no cliff is too steep to scale
Even in life's most tumultuous storms
One can feel sheltered, safe, and all warm

We were born to be loved and connected
Not to feel inadequate or rejected
When we feel we completely belong
Then we will no longer yearn or long

To be utterly and completely loved
Is a gift alone from Heaven above
It is when we join God in holy communion
His unconditional love forms this perfect union.

The Lord your God is with you, the Mighty Warrior who saves. He will take great delight
in you; in his love he will no longer rebuke you, but will rejoice over you with singing.

ZEPHANIAH 3:17

YOU WALKED AWAY

THERE CAN BE A DARK, PAINFUL side of love, the kind that brings hurt and disappointment when we suffer its loss. This other side of love is heartbreak and unrequited love. When we suffer a broken heart with no options to regain the object of our love, how do we survive? How do we go on?

We can move forward by turning to the *source* of love. God is the only one who can soften and assuage the pain. All human relationships, at some point, bring disappointment because we are imperfect human beings, but God is perfect and will never forsake us. We'll come to see that our internal emptiness can never be fully filled with human love; only God's love will fill and satisfy us completely.

My heart was shattered, torn, left bleeding
It was only you that I was needing

You Walked Away

You walked away
Although I begged you to stay
You left me in shambles with no words left to say

My heart was shattered, torn, left bleeding
It was only you that I was needing
I was desperate, frantic, forced into conceding

How to survive and go on breathing?
When my heart wants to just stop beating
This despair has left me broken and seething

Alone again, forlorn again
By myself to aimlessly roam again
To find my way, some way back home again

Lost without a compass or any direction
There can be no reprieve or any concession
To find a moment's relief, I would give all
    my possessions

So where do I seek my comfort and hope to once
    again sing?
It is only God who can remove this bitter, biting sting
It is only He, for to me solace He brings

So even though you walked away
And I begged you to stay
God did not forsake me, He showed me my way.

Never will I leave you; never will I forsake you.

HEBREWS 13:5

DID I KNOW?

IN THIS POEM, I CONTINUE TO reflect on the darker side of love. Sometimes, we slip into relationships and situations that can damage our lives and the lives and feelings of others. This could be a person who is an old heart's desire or someone with whom we have immediate, unexplained chemistry and connection. Before we are totally aware of it, we may have crossed over into a space where we don't belong.

This darker side of love is not sanctioned by God. It will never bring us where we should be or where God wants us to be. It is forcing something God has not intended, and it eventually leads to disappointment, hurt, and heartbreak. We then come to wonder why our minds did not protect us or warn us. Or did we just not listen? Did we know what we were doing?

Paul, in Romans 7, struggles with sin, doing something that he knows is wrong. He doesn't want to give in, but he does it anyway. Just like Paul, we are frail creatures with even frailer strength of will. Only with God can we find our strength and courage to conquer the challenges we face each and every day.

Did I know this love could never now be?
Did my emptiness fill briefly,
but now the void to see?

Did I Know?

Did my heart know your words were futile?
Did my logic know your actions would be brutal?

Did my judgment feel the danger that we tread?
Did my intuition sense to pull away, not to be led?

Did my ears hear the words that had no meaning?
Did my eyes see only a vapid specter fleeting?

Did my touch feel only what had once been?
Did my lips linger longer, denying this sin?

Did my perception construe the lost years as new?
Did my mind process the sweet promises as untrue?

Did my body acknowledge its yearning was from
*   lost years?*

Did my trust decide to surrender all of my fears?

Did my conscience reflect and acknowledge the blame?
Did my feelings neglect to know the shame?

Did my emotions get confused thinking I could wait?
Did my soul realize it was already too late?

Did I know this love could never now be?
Did my emptiness fill briefly, but now the void to see?

Did I know fully this would be all pretend?
Did my spirit whisper you are here once again?

Did I know all along it would finally end?
For without God's sanction, together we could
*   never win.*

But as for me, I watch in hope for the Lord, I wait for God my Savior; my God will
hear me. Do not gloat over me, my enemy! . . . Though I sit in darkness, the Lord will
be my light. Because I have sinned against him, I will bear the Lord's wrath, until he
pleads my case. . . . He will bring me out into the light; I will see his righteousness.

MICAH 7:7–9

BOTH SIDES OF LOVE

LOVE ALWAYS HAS TWO SIDES. WHEN we deeply love, loss, hurt, and pain are always a risk. But it is always worth continuing to love. Love is what makes us truly human, joining us to one another.

I have been on both sides of love in my life. I know the deep pain of heartbreak and the compassionate sadness one feels when pain is inflicted on someone else after love diminishes. Yet love gives us life, and it gives life to others. It is what connects us to others and to God, as God is love. So, we must never stop loving.

False pretensions and deceitful illusions
Make for love's turmoil and confusions

Both Sides of Love

I have known love on both sides
Heartbreaker and painful heartbreak rides
I have heard excuses, falsehoods, and lies
I know deep hurt that has made me cry

False pretensions and deceitful illusions
Make for love's turmoil and confusions
Love is just given with no constraints or control
It cannot be contrived, bought, or sold

I have wished I could kindle desire's fire
But trying and trying will make one a liar
Seeing another suffering, hurt, and lost
Is tearful and painful to bear this cost

A broken heart with too many pieces and cracks

Then no mending or repair; one can't go back
The facts and truth still constantly remain
The battle wounds and spillage cannot be contained

Innocent casualties left in the ruins are unfair
Despite these dire consequences one can still care
Sacrifice, denial becomes the price; it's worth
Whatever it takes to stop the pain and hurt

Only with God can one find wholeness and healing
To have felt both sides, to know these feelings
Compassion, understanding to continue loving,
  our hearts to give
Love is worth all these risks; it is why
  we continue to live.

Whoever does not love does not know God, because God is love.

1 JOHN 4:8

EVERGREEN EVERMORE

WHAT IS REAL LOVE? IT IS constant, unchanging, and everlasting. Like the evergreen trees that never change, remaining green, lush, and full of life, that is what love is and should be for us. God allows love to endure the impossible, so it remains steadfast. We can lean on Him to heal and restore our relationships.

As humans, we are imperfect, and we will fail each other. All human relationships will disappoint sooner or later. Marriages fail at an alarming rate because of these deep hurts and failures. What would it mean if we could heal those damaged relationships and mend our broken hearts? Such a task may seem impossible for us, but what is impossible for humans is always possible with God.

I am suggesting that we allow God to restore and heal our broken relationships. Just think what this could mean to all our loved ones when we decide to forgive and allow amends to be made.

I wrote the poem "Evergreen Evermore" with these thoughts in mind.

It is what lasts and
remains into our core
Through the centuries, it
has been mankind's lore

23

Evergreen Evermore

Love is Evergreen Evermore
Our hearts can then take flight and soar
It is what lasts and remains into our core
Through the centuries, it has been
  mankind's lore

This is love that endures
It is steadfast and makes us sure

Obstacles will get in the way
Through the unknown wilderness, we
  can still play
Knowing we will make it through
  each day
Together, forever bonded we will stay

Unquenchable lasting desire
Is what keeps stoking our ongoing fire

Broken hearts are ours to mend
Forgiveness and mercy we each send
The love we share will not, shall not end
Excused transgressions no longer offend

That unquantifiable chemistry and attraction
Are what draws us to mutual pleasure
  and satisfaction

Though darkness looms always near
Our hands together, we will not fear
Although deep wounding cuts still sear

Our shared love we will hold dear
Two melded souls into one
From this love we cannot run

Eternal, everlasting love will win
Our progeny links and knits us forever kin
Sacrifice and honor dwells somewhere within
Commitment and trust can live on after sin

Our marriage covenant cannot be broken
So words of forgiveness and love must
  be spoken

Love is Evergreen Evermore
Our hearts burn with a blazing roar
Love's wellspring flows again once more
Mended hearts can still forever adore

True adoration from God above
Is our model for human love

What is impossible for man, let go
There are some things that only God
  can sow
When we feel hopeless, discouraged, and low
Turn to God to make all things possible;
  this He will show

So it is in the giving and forgiving
That allow us, imperfect souls, to continue
  loving and go on living.

Love is patient, love is kind. It does not envy,
it does not boast, it is not proud.

1 CORINTHIANS 13:4

ON MARRIAGE

I WROTE A POEM TO EXPRESS THE things that I have found to be important in an enduring marriage. A marriage will have some troubles and challenges, but when God is your strength and glue, then your relationship can withstand the trials. When we place God at the center of marriage—just as the three-stranded cord is stronger than the two-stranded cord—it is not easily broken. It can last through tension, not breaking. When we build our house on solid bedrock, not sand, our home will not sink and vanish. So, as we build our marriages on God, they will endure, withstanding all storms.

*Putting ourselves after the needs of the other
That's what it takes to love one another*

On Marriage

Marriage is a like a three-legged stool
God at the center is the golden rule
Otherwise, it cannot firmly stand
It will collapse with nowhere to land

Marriage is not just giving fifty percent
One hundred percent is what needs to be sent
Putting ourselves after the needs of the other
That's what it takes to love one another

Marriage is arm in arm being skin to skin
Conjugal intimacy is built from within
This closeness is what helps hearts to blend
If not, it's just hollow motions and notions, all pretend

Marriage is to cherish and honor with a gentle touch
It is to this love and acceptance that we clutch
When we acknowledge and feel the other's pain,
Empathy and validation become the foremost gain

Marriage is to be placed first, with God only above
This connubial model is a gift of love
Lasting bonds form a strong, steadfast union
Then our allegiance will never know any confusion

Marriage is with God as it does first begin
With Him at the center it will endure to the end
Our vows and promises were not meant to bend
This is the marital message God wants to send Amen.

✝

Two are better than one, because they have a good return for their labor: If either of
them falls down, one can help the other up. But pity anyone who falls and has no one
to help them up. Also, if two lie down together, they will keep warm. But how can
one keep warm alone? Though one may be overpowered, two can defend themselves.
A cord of three strands is not quickly broken.

ECCLESIASTES 4:9–12

FORGIVENESS

FORGIVENESS IS A GIFT YOU GIVE to another person, but it is also a gift you give to yourself. Forgiveness gives you freedom by removing the power held over you that can block your peace and joy. The gift of forgiveness is freedom, and the gift of freedom is peace. Peace then opens the door to joy so it may enter your life once again.

This does not mean the actions that hurt you are ever condoned or excused, but by choosing to forgive, you release yourself from the bondage of pain and suffering that can dominate your life. The gifts received are freedom, peace, and joy.

Forgiveness is not about
keeping the score
It's about loving and
giving even more

Forgiveness

Forgiveness is what heals
But it can be so difficult to feel

Pride is the obstacle one must get past
Ego blocks the gate so very fast

When winning becomes the game
It will inflict the most pain with shame

Forgiveness is not about keeping the score
It's about loving and giving even more

Forgiving does not mean excusing
It does mean to stop accusing

You will probably never forget the hurt
But forgiving can rebuild your self-worth

Humility is fed by love and care
It knows forgiveness will not make it fair

Forgiveness is the price of freedom's way
Retaliation of the hurt will never pay

Forgiveness may not be deserved
But loving relationships it can preserve

It can spare others so much hurt
But it means you will not be put first

Forgiveness, from bondage it will free
Releasing the words of hurt you feel and see

Finally letting go of all the pain

Allows freedom and peace to remain

It means joy can come back in
To feel happiness once more again

Forgiveness becomes a choice to choose
It does mean you will surrender, but not lose

It's a chance you have to take
Because waiting may make it too late

Then one's heart can be lost
When you are not willing to bear the cost

Trust must be restored
It is what will heal the pain and discord

The forgiveness you receive by God's grace
Is love and mercy for man's unmerited case

So as you receive forgiveness, freely to give
Then the choice becomes how you want to live

Love will be the heart's only cure
When healing happens you will know for sure

Forgiveness is a gift you give to yourself
It will provide you with life's genuine wealth

It is a gift of all gifts
Hurt and pain are what it lifts

To know the gift of forgiveness
Is to receive the heart's most loving kiss.

Be kind and compassionate to one another, forgiving each other,
just as in Christ God forgave you.

EPHESIANS 4:32

REFLECTIONS IN A
MIRRORED GLASS

OUTSIDE APPEARANCES ARE SO DECEIVING. BUT it's in our eyes that God's light and love shines out for the world to see. I wrote this poem as I was thinking about the differences between people's outside looks and how how they are on the inside.

Appearances can certainly deceive others, but we can never deceive our God. He knows our hearts and true motivations. So never be quick to judge people. Instead, look for their shining light.

Let our hearts be a light for
all the world to see
That is God's desire and
plan for you and me

Reflections in a Mirrored Glass

I see the reflection in the mirrored glass
What I see on the surface will not last
But I see a child of wonder within,
Who remains my closest trusted friend
But it is He who knows me in and out
And loves me as I am, without a doubt
He accepts me with all my mistakes
Just as He has felt all my painful heartbreaks

God, You see my gentle kind face
While knowing all my sin and disgrace
I still remain your precious child
You continue to love me someway, somehow
You keep teaching me and I keep learning
All the while I am becoming more discerning
One day I hope to be
The person you planned and wanted for me

On the outside others may perceive

Someone that looks confident and carefree
But does the inner light shine out?
It is all glory to God I want to shout
Not false perceptions, as looks can deceive
They will never lead me to salvation or reprieve
It's God's love that must overflow
From the inside out for others to know

Don't judge with a glance when we see each other
Because it is about loving and caring for one another
Let our hearts be a light for all the world to see
That is God's desire and plan for you and me
We may not understand while on earth we live
But in the dark valleys, all our trust to God
   we must give
So in the mirrored reflections we only see partly
For now we see through the glass darkly.

You are the light of the world. A town built on a hill cannot be hidden. Neither do
people light a lamp and put it under a bowl. Instead they put it on its stand, and it
gives light to everyone in the house. In the same way, let your light shine before oth-
ers, that they may see your good deeds and glorify your Father in heaven.

MATTHEW 5:14–16

HOUSE OF THE SOUL

OUR SOULS ARE WHAT FORM OUR personhood, which is who we truly are. Our physical bodies can be deceiving and certainly do not represent the kind of person we are. So, we all must look deeper and beyond the superficial to really see and know an individual and all people.

The truth is our physical bodies are temporary housing for our eternal souls as we make this brief sojourn here on planet Earth. We grow, mature, and learn, developing into something new. Hopefully that is enough to cross God's finish line well. The fact is, we have a choice and are free to choose our eternal destiny. Thankfully, we have a loving, forgiving God who knows and sees our true hearts.

The body is a house of the soul
The true self lives within and unfolds

35

House of the Soul

The body is a house of the soul
The true self lives within and unfolds

Body boxes are made to contain and hide
Emotions and feelings swelter, lurking inside

Outside stereotypes and prejudices are not right
Delusive, external witnesses without true sight

Glistening eyes are openings into the soul
Translucent windows are their major role

Light shines out from goodness within
But darkness will throw shadows from stealthy sin

Beguiling body houses are all dressed to conceal
Cursory, quick glances will never reveal

Pretty outside, smiling, all adorned
Can hide broken souls, doleful and forlorn

Shades of gray, harrowed hints of hurt and scorn
Exterior false illusions can mock hearts that mourn

Trapped inside, this prisoner wants to be free
So do not falsely judge or think you really see

Life is the gift for spiritual growth and insight
Death is the friend who puts souls to flight

Prickly senses sear through into the soul's room
Bring mixed emotions where tears of grief's losses
    always loom

Training-ground terrain for our future fate
Lessons learned in time to make death's date

What lies within the long or short dash
It's up to us what we will leave and make last

Soul houses, temporary perishing abodes
It's the choices taken and which roads

True character choices do shape and mold
Nothing is excused, even mistakes untold

Life is short; it's your fate and mine to cast
Each present moment ticking quickly becomes the past

Reason and logic may help mundane wins
But compassion and faith lead to heavenly ends

Passion and lust are body house rules
Sensual desire loses, will makes us fools

The body boxes can hold God's sublime gifts
So what will come out when the top finally lifts?

Houses of souls where furtive secrets may hide
God sees all that is within, hidden deep inside

Our eternal future is for us to decide
So the crux is both—our final destination and
    this life's ride.

So we fix our eyes not on what is seen, but on what is unseen, since what is seen
is temporary, but what is unseen is eternal.

2 CORINTHIANS 4:18

CONNECTION

I WROTE THIS POEM BECAUSE I BELIEVE that connecting with God and others is our core meaning and purpose in life. As the old saying goes, "No one is an island." We were meant to love and be loved. Let us turn toward God and embrace that which He created us to be, fully connected to others and to Him.

Thanksgiving represents goodwill, fellowship, community, and connection between people. It is a time to embrace family and others and to give thanks to God for all our blessings. Let's celebrate today, and every day, this tradition of Thanksgiving. God's blessings to all!

What gives us life and breath
is our connection to others
It defines our humanness,
loving one another

Connection

What gives us life and breath is our connection
    to others
It defines our humanness, loving one another
It stirs movement within our souls and being
It is what it means for our hearts to be
    deeply seeing

Connection is a risky, precarious notion
Timing and fate can halt with a memory
    as the lone token
Hurt and loss may be the binding cost
Then fractured lives scattered can be lost

What could have been, would or should
    have been
To replay mistaken actions all over again
Remains a drifting, imaginary thought
Leaves hearts hurting and distraught

Created stories play in our hazy dreams
Nothing can be changed with trickery
    or schemes
Reality is relationships, all lost and torn
The remaining results are rejection and scorn

But our every cell longs for intimate union
Connection is about community, commitment,
    and communion
We were made to connect with deep bond
It so much more than just feelings of being fond

Connection expects transparency, nothing false
Openness and truth becomes it all
Then trust and closeness can prevail
But vulnerability can't be prevented to no avail

Connection gives our lives promise and meaning
It is what keeps us breathing and our
    hearts beating
It is for a glimmer of significance we search
    and seek
Then our future can become hopeful, not bleak

It is connection that defines our humanity
Being without it can lead mankind to insanity
God made us this way in His image
Otherwise, this journey would be a strange,
    lone pilgrimage

Dear friends, let us love one another, for love comes from God.

1 JOHN 4:7

THIS THING CALLED LOVE

WHEN GOD CREATED MAN AND WOMAN, He gave us romantic (eros) love. This bond between two people has inspired great literature and torn nations apart. It is almost like a chemical reaction with an unknown formula. This poem, "This Thing Called Love," is written to portray the complexity of love as it also has its shadowy side. I have known this spectrum in my life as I've experienced deep love along with deep hurt and heartbreak. Despite the risk of hurt and pain, it is always worth continuing to give and receive love. Loving is a core need and part of our humanity. God created us to love. We love because God first loved us. It connects us to the source of all love, as He is the wellspring of love. God is love.

It is about sacrifice,
patience, and forgiving
It is what keeps us
breathing and living.

This Thing Called Love

What is this thing called love?
God only knows from Heaven above
It can't be explained
It can drive us insane

It is impossible to withhold
Our character it can change and mold
As much as we try to deny
It breaks hearts, makes us cry

How many have fallen to sin?
The cause was love in the end
Passion, desire, wants, and lust
It can lead to breaking all trust

Shattered hearts can leave lives broken
When we are not the one who was chosen
When two hearts become tightly bound
This is the solace longing to be found

Why does love have such control?
For it, souls to the devil have been sold
We risk all, knowing the cost
We wager, not caring what's lost

Once it's given there is no return
Something our hearts never seem to learn
It can make us weak or strong
We can't let go; it keeps us hanging on

Does it ever leave its hold?
What remains can find lost hearts cold

It can fill us with sadness and depression
It can drive us crazed with obsession

Hurt and loss, happiness and bliss
This is what we always risk
But love is what matters in the end
Broken hearts can always mend

Are we just pawns being played?
Our future fate may be cast and laid
Just for a stolen, stealthy, tender kiss
Knowing this touch and feeling will be missed

Melded hearts of true soulmates
Remind us love is never too late
Frail humans are what we are
It is love that will last, carrying us far

What is this thing called love?
God only knows from Heaven above
It is about sacrifice, patience, and forgiving
It is what keeps us breathing and living

Love is what connects us to God and each other
It is also about loving all, as sisters and brothers
Given as a divine gift to be our energy
  and life force
From God, the eternal wellspring of love;
  its original source.

We love because he first loved us.

1 John 4:19

SHE

MY YOUNGEST DAUGHTER GOT MARRIED ON Saturday, December 19, 2015. This poem was a wedding gift for her and a recovery gift for my other daughter to remind them that a woman of God lives life fully and joyfully with a heart overflowing with love. I want all of us to strive to be this amazing "She." My oldest daughter says this is now her favorite poem, and she likes to read it every morning to remind her of who she wants to be: this "She," a woman walking in God's grace and light, spreading joy and love to everyone in her path.

She knows that life is led by
God's calling
So she is brave and strong; she
never fears falling

44

She

She moves with passion and such joy
Sowing gladness and love, while remaining coy

Her heart flows with giving and is full of lust
She knows no limits; love is a must

Her spirit longs to run and be free
She feels with intensity, just to be

She humbly serves others with love and grace
She preaches the Gospel and her sweet
  Jesus's case

She works to change the imperfect present world
Hoping to bind perfection to the future all furled

Her kindness and gentleness are her soft touch
She gives and loves always, much too much

Her heart can be worn on the edge of her sleeve
Once she gives her love, it will never leave

She throws and casts fate all away
Living and challenging her life day by day

She seizes each moment as it might be her last
As she knows time is speeding by way too fast

She knows that life is led by God's calling
So she is brave and strong; she never fears falling

Her God rules her heart; He's her strength and
  her might
This is what gives her the courage to fight

She interacts and lives her life feeling deeply
Her inner intuitive voice leads her completely

Her ethereal light shines on others' ways
Her eyes and her smile glow as bright sunny rays

Her empathic presence is like a warm summer day
Her inner child within delights to laugh and
  to play

Can this nymph of light, this mysterious She,
  possibly ever hope to be me?

This is my prayer and my wish to see
I trust God; He can help make me to be.

✝

"For I know the plans I have for you," declares the Lord, "plans to prosper you and
not to harm you, plans to give you hope and a future."

JEREMIAH 29:11

GOD'S MUSE

I WROTE MY POEM "GOD'S MUSE" TO express my gratitude and appreciation to God for His abiding, unwavering love. It was written as a thank-you for growing Healing Presence Ministry to followers all over the world reading my poetry about God's love. What I have witnessed in my ministry has testified to me of the power of God to do the miraculous. I know what has happened is not about me; it is only about God. So, I see myself as God's servant or His scribe. I also hope I am His muse, giving Him joy and pleasure as my words bring Him glory and praise.

*He is my Savior and
gives me life
I will never fear or
fail to do His fight*

God's Muse

My heart sings and longs to be
Servant of my Savior to make of me

To love Him I so do wish
Yearning to feel His tender, fatherly kiss

To please Him and bring Him delight
Sends my soul to take flight

He is so strong, powerful with might
It is He who gives my heart's insight

Intuition and inspiration His voice within
Whispers to me what messages to send

For others to know and feel His love
Is always pleasing to our God above

He calls on me for His things to do
I first resist, but then I always ensue

I have surrendered my mundane views
He is only what my heart pursues

It is He who makes me safe and secure
He always waits patiently with His
   tender, loving allure

Whatever He sends I have become willing
My old worldly ways have met their
   final killing

I look to God to lead my journey straight
With Him faith and belief can never be too late

He is always there to extend His merciful grace
Jesus alone can and will plead my
   unmerited case

He leads me down unknown, untrodden paths
I know now I will never fear God's final
   judgment or wrath

He is my Savior and gives me life
I will never fear or fail to do His fight

I am His vessel and His tool
My heart alone He completely rules

So I choose each day to be God's devoted muse
I am His now and forever to dutifully use.

✝

The Lord makes firm the steps of the one who delights in him; though he may
stumble, he will not fall, for the Lord upholds him with his hand.

PSALM 37:23–24

BE KIND

ESOP, JESUS, MOTHER TERESA, AND MAYA Angelou (to name a few) remind us to be kind to one another. Kindness is defined as the act of being friendly, generous, and considerate. Kindness can be described by affection, warmth, gentleness, concern, care, compassion, and warm-heartedness. Kindness requires intentionality because it is not a passive trait. It is a choice to be kind, and it is always the right choice.

In a world full of violence, suffering, and inequality, it has become increasingly important to be kind to our fellow humans. It seems such a simple gesture that requires little effort, but this act may at times require great courage and strength to reach out to another with benevolence. If each one of us made this effort, together we could make the world a better place. So be kind.

*Remember God's gift of
unmerited love
Is ours alone, given from
Heaven above*

Be Kind

When a wrong is done that you don't understand
Know that what matters is which side you land
So be Kind

Know that others may be suffering deep hurt and loss
We will never know what they have experienced
  and the cost
So be Kind

Open your heart to those with less
There may be so many things they may have missed
So be Kind

Some dreams are wished upon a star
But other dreams remain remote, distant and very far
So be Kind

If feelings and emotions are angry and terse
Remember to still try to place others first
So be Kind

Always give mercy, forgiveness, and grace
Don't be concerned what others think and
  with saving face
So be Kind

No one knows what suffering and pain
Lies undetected, driving another nearly insane
So be Kind

Hearts torn, all broken and in quiet desperation
Make for severe actions without contemplation
So be Kind

Remember God's gift of unmerited love
Is ours alone, given from Heaven above
So be Kind.

A new command I give you: Love one another. As I have loved you, so you must love one
another. By this everyone will know that you are my disciples, if you love one another.

JOHN 13:34–35

REPENTANCE

W E REPENT BECAUSE WE LOVE GOD and desire to please Him. Repentance allows for God's forgiveness. He knows your heart, so you can't pretend. Repentance and forgiveness are intricately tied together. This kind of forgiveness is a gift you give yourself to free yourself from bondage. God's forgiveness is founded on the condition of your heart. I am confident that if you have a truly repentant heart, there is no sin so great that God won't forgive it. And yes, that means even murderers and the like. If they come to faith and have true repentance, they will be forgiven.

If we have sinned once, even a little sin, we cannot enter Heaven. All of our sins must be forgiven. I, for one, know I am a sinner and live in a glass house. But God, in His love and mercy, offers all of us forgiveness when we stand before Him with a repentant heart. It can sometimes be more difficult to forgive yourself than to forgive others, although God forgives you for any sin you bring to Him. If God can extend undeserved mercy and forgiveness to you, should you not do the same for yourself? It is never too late to repent, even up to our last breath. Praise God for His love and mercy!

*Repentance comes from
deep in one's soul
It acknowledges and
accepts your full role*

Repentance

Repentance comes from deep in one's soul
It acknowledges and accepts your full role
Forgiveness becomes possible because of repentance
Then there will no longer be a condemned sentence

Repentance means you can finally make amends
When you recognize and accept all your sins
It wipes away, cleaning your slate
Bringing you to a more righteous fate

Repentance means you truly care
But does not mean it will ever make it fair
It's letting go of the reasons why
Going to God to accept and not deny

Repentance means that you do feel regret
Now no reason for deceit, lies, and fret
It is the humble, straight path cast
That can allow your loving relationships to last

Repentance is about feeling remorse
It will lead you down a more faithful course
The relationship with God it will restore
It's about loving Him and caring even more

Repentance, broken bridges it will suspend
Loving-kindness and caring it will send
In the mirror you see your frail, human face
Knowing you need God's mercy and grace

Repentance is also about nonjudgment of others
When empathy and mercy become your druthers
Broken hearts it will mend
The shame and guilt will finally expend

Repentance requires humility in you to be
It will bend you and take you to your knee
You may hit the hard wall
And off your high pedestal you will fall

Repentance is accepting your guilt
Being deeply sorry allows trust to be rebuilt
For forgiveness, repentance is the key
Then gone are your transgressions, setting you free

Repentance can be a long, rocky road
But it will relieve the heavy, burdensome load
It allows you to make a fresh start
When God sees and knows your true heart

Repentance allows God's forgiveness to come within
It determines eternity, where you will end
God you will no longer offend
A message of love and mercy He will extend

Repentance before God of your sin
Begins for you a brand-new life again
Your repentance enables God to forgive
It means you can be in Christ and fully live.

Repent, then, and turn to God, so that your sins may be wiped out.

ACTS 3:19

PART TWO

God's Love

THE DIVINE PARADOX

"THE DIVINE PARADOX" WAS WRITTEN AS an expression of love and gratitude for how God changes us into a new creation. He wastes nothing, not even a single teardrop, in using all our experiences to grow us and transform us.

In losing our life we find
The Life.
In the paradox of faith
we are transformed.

The Divine Paradox

In giving we receive.
In loving we are loved.
In losing we gain.
In surrender we are victorious.
In dying we are born.
In forgiving we are forgiven.
In accepting we are accepted.
In death we find life.
In weakness we find strength.
In quiet we find music.
In letting go we are saved.

In pain we are healed.
In suffering we are restored.
In brokenness we are mended.
In pruning we grow.
In emptying we are filled.
In submission we find power.
In darkness we find light.
In mystery we find understanding.
In stillness we find God.
In losing our life we find The Life.
In the paradox of faith we are transformed.

Therefore, if anyone is in Christ, the new creation has come:
The old has gone, the new is here!

2 CORINTHIANS 5:17

BELOVED

NOT EVERYONE HAS A LOVING, SUPPORTIVE father. Many of us do not have an earthly father to exemplify how our Heavenly Father loves us. My father struggled with depression and alcoholism, and my parents divorced when I was five years old. His alcoholism deeply affected our relationship and my ability to be close to him. He has been deceased for many years, but I know if he ever loved anyone in this world, he loved me.

My earthly father may have failed me in many ways, but I know unconditional fatherly love because of God's care for me. I also see it in my husband's eyes and actions as he loves our children. I know that God is my Father, and I am His beloved. I wrote the poem "Beloved" with these thoughts in mind.

He makes me feel special
and I have His favor
With Him living in me I
know I am braver

61

Beloved

God is my Father, and I am His beloved
He is with me always, giving me His love

Although I remain undeserving and a sinner I be
He has sent His precious Son to suffer and die
 for me

He corrects me with love even though I err
This unconditional love of His remains so rare

I always fall short of what He has planned
But He allows me time to do all that I can

God provides when I don't even know
He is always there to pick me up when I am
 feeling low

He guides me down the path I must go
He is patient when I am moving way too slow

He whispers through the still small voice that
 lives in my head

He speaks to me through dreams while I am
 tucked safe in my bed

He gives me the strength, peace, and rest
 that I need
Nurture and nourishment, He provides
 and feeds

I hear and see Him by being in Nature
I have placed all my bets on Pascal's wager

He makes me feel special and I have His favor
With Him living in me I know I am braver

He is a good Father always being fair
I know in my heart He will forever care

I am His beloved and He is my Father
I give to Him all my heart and soul with ardor.

I will be a Father to you, and you will be my sons and daughters, says the Lord Almighty.

2 CORINTHIANS 6:18

HOME

WHAT IS IT ABOUT THE WORD *home* that brings up such thoughts and feelings of safety and contentment? Images of saved memories in our minds will make us smile and bring a sense of longing deep within us. This is what my poem "Home" addresses.

Where is our home really? It's not actually a place or destination. It is carried in our hearts. It is where love lives. God is pure love, and God is our home.

*The fires and hot embers
radiate bright light
Consolation and comfort they
bring into the dark night*

Home

Home again, take me home
I no longer want to flounder and roam

That warm, safe place
That brings a satisfied smile to my face

Where I am known and accepted
Never feeling inept or rejected

The fires and hot embers radiate bright light
Consolation and comfort they bring into the dark night

Flames burning, reflections dancing on the walls
Fond past memories in my mind they recall

Contentment, trust, joy, and peace
At home these feelings never cease

Home is the Heart where Love lives
God is Love, so Home is wherever God is.

No one has ever seen God; but if we love one another, God
lives in us and his love is made complete in us.

1 JOHN 4:12

IN THIS HOLY PLACE

I VISITED A CENTURY-OLD CHURCH IN FRANCE. The stone pillars and arching ceiling were immense. The man made structure was an architectural feat. As I quietly sat among the breathtaking grandeur of the church, my eyes seized on the huge crucifix of our suffering Savior, God, as a man, who came willingly to give His life.

As I stared at Christ, I was overtaken by His sacrifice, a pure gift of love. I saw the pain and suffering in His sad eyes and slumped body. My eyes filled with tears—liquid prayers of gratitude and thanksgiving that He died for me, so I might be set free.

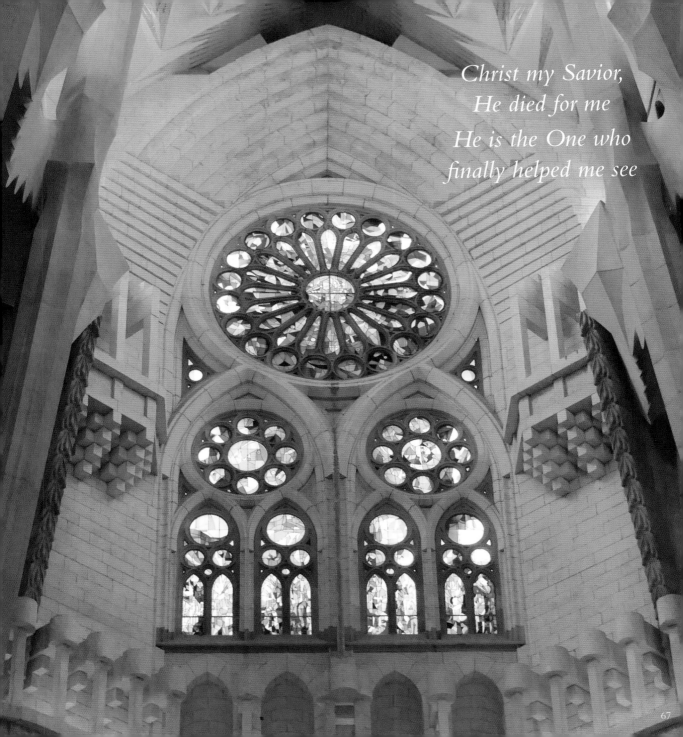

Christic my Savior,
He died for me
He is the One who
finally helped me see

In This Holy Place

In this holy place
Somewhere far away you take
As if floating on a still quiet lake
Tears in my eyes His suffering makes

Christ my Savior, He died for me
He is the One who finally helped me see
I am no longer afraid and need to flee
I rest with who I am, to just be

Freedom lives in His sacrifice
His death the payment does suffice
No longer in my heart is fear or strife
No longer do I wear a mask or disguise

Now the Holy Spirit will remain near
With Him so close I have no fears
On my heart His love is permanently seared
I now have eyes that see and ears that hear
Amen.

But he has appeared once for all at the culmination of the ages to do away with sin by the sacrifice of himself. Just as people are destined to die once, and after that to face judgment, so Christ was sacrificed once to take away the sins of many; and he will appear a second time, not to bear sin, but to bring salvation to those who are waiting for him.

HEBREWS 9:26—28

WAITING IS A GOD GAME

EVERY SINGLE DAY, I AM THANKFUL for my merciful, ever-patient God who continues to love me, never giving up on me as He waits on me to get it right.

I am the impatient type who wants things to happen on my time. God has His own timing and plans for us. As I have grown older, one of the most important lessons God has taught me is patience. This really goes back to trusting God. Sometimes, we just have to wait and be still to hear God and His plan for us. Waiting is a God Game.

Waiting is an art I must learn
Waiting is a gift to help discern

Waiting Is a God Game

Waiting is a God Game
Waiting leads me down the long lane

Waiting teaches me the virtue I need to know
Waiting can help me to let go

Waiting is so hard for me to do
Waiting enough will reveal the clue

Waiting I need to embrace
Waiting will lead me to God's grace

Waiting lets God sow
Waiting allows the time to grow

Waiting is an art I must learn

Waiting is a gift to help discern

Waiting is putting my life on hold
Waiting is used by God to mold

Waiting will not leave me the same
Waiting on God helps me contain

Waiting keeps me from passing God
Waiting reveals God's path to trod

Waiting is the patience to see God's time
Waiting holds the tension that is mine

Waiting tells me to be silent and still
Waiting allows me to see God's will.

Whether you turn to the right or to the left, your ears will hear
a voice behind you, saying, "This is the way; walk in it."

Isaiah 30:21

THE PRAYER OF THE
WANDERING SHEEP

I WROTE THIS POEM AS A PRAYER for myself and others who stray
and wander off course. Although I wander, I know my way back, and I know who
my Good Shepherd is. I am so grateful every day for God's love, grace, and mercy.
At times, I must try God's patience as He watches me make the same mistakes over and
over again. I imagine Him rolling His eyes as He sees me in this cycle of repetition,
thinking, "There she goes again. You'd think she would have learned by now." But He
is there waiting to guide me back on the path He has destined for me.

The sinner I am would remain forever lost
I am only saved at Your sacrifice and cost

The Prayer of the Wandering Sheep

My heart opens up and sings
I wait patiently to see what You bring

You inflow, filling my soul
Once again You guide me back to Your fold

I wander like a lost sheep
I repent once again and I weep

Your loving-kindness grants me Your grace
My spirit so yearns to see Your sweet face

I trust You to show me the way
I pray, dear Lord, don't let me stray

Help me to see my path You chose
I praise and thank God for the day You rose

The sinner I am would remain forever lost
I am only saved at Your sacrifice and cost

Release me from bondage to fly free like a dove
Blessed am I to know Your eternal, everlasting love
Amen.

Then Jesus told them this parable: "Suppose one of you has a hundred sheep and loses one of them. Doesn't he leave the ninety-nine in the open country and go after the lost sheep until he finds it? And when he finds it, he joyfully puts it on his shoulders and goes home. Then he calls his friends and neighbors together and says, 'Rejoice with me; I have found my lost sheep.' I tell you that in the same way there will be more rejoicing in heaven over one sinner who repents than over ninety-nine righteous persons who do not need to repent."

LUKE 15:3–7

CONSEQUENCES

I HAVE WRITTEN THIS POEM, "CONSEQUENCES," TO empha-
size how important each decision we make can be, with effects we may never
have anticipated. We are free to make our own choices but not to choose the
consequences of those choices.

Although we make mistakes and suffer consequences, God still is faithful in His
love for us. Let us all be more mindful of the consequences our decisions can produce.
The only real way to be confident in our choices is to be prayerful with each one and
to trust God each and every day.

It is from our own selves
God wants to protect
So be mindful and prayerful
of how our choices can affect

Consequences

Choices bring consequences that may be dire
Once chosen they can ignite a raging fire
No redoing, looking, or taking back
Consequences can easily throw us off track

We are free to make the initial choice
But consequences can later take our voice
We cannot determine what follows then
Consequences might be our calamity, not
　our friend

So every action must be carefully perceived
　and thought
As our final resolve may leave us distraught
Each decision may become a learning lesson
Consequences teach and may become a
　reckoning session

So there is a reason for God's commandments
　and rules
And doing unto others as we were taught in school
It is from our own selves God wants to protect
So be mindful and prayerful of how our choices
　can affect

God loves us deeply to our essence and core
No person on earth could love us more
It is from the consequences of our own choices
　He wants to save
In the end, it is only through the gift of
　His Son, whom God freely gave.

Trust in the Lord with all your heart and lean not on your own understanding; in all your
ways submit to him, and he will make your paths straight.

PROVERBS 3:5–6

REDEMPTION

I WANTED TO REFLECT ON WHAT IT means to be redeemed, to be forgiven and transformed, to be made new. Redemption cleans and purifies something that is soiled, making it new and good again. God can redeem any situation and any person. Even our deepest sin can be redeemed. This gives us hope because there can always be a new beginning with redemption.

*Trials and tribulations I can
now withstand
Into my Savior's arms I will
always land*

Redemption

What does it mean to know redemption?
It means God takes away all and every contention
No matter the allegations, they are wiped clean
His blood covers me as I stand before the King
My heart is now free from repression
There is no longer any sinful obsession

He turns the bad in me into good
All things are made right as they should
He sees my soul and knows all
He leads me down my path with His call
I know my Redeemer lives
It is eternal life to me He gives

This blessing is undeserved
In gratitude to Him all my life I will serve
It is Jesus who has already for me atoned
He is the one beside God on Heaven's throne
He extends to me His unmerited grace
My transgressions I now do not face

I was sinking in sin and was to drown
Before I was lost; now I am found
With repentance I am now exempt
There is no longer any future contempt
I am no longer one of the lost and fallen
I am now His to forever call on

Trials and tribulations I can now withstand
Into my Savior's arms I will always land
What He has planned for me I cannot imagine
    or conceive
He has given me His forgiveness and reprieve
The best is now yet to come
Because in my heart forever lives the Son

I am redeemed, I am redeemed
No matter how it might or may seem
I am for an eternity all His
This will be from now on and now is
Praise God, I will give Him thanks forever
My soul will not leave Him, no, never.

In him we have redemption through his blood, the forgiveness
of sins, in accordance with the riches of God's grace.

EPHESIANS 1:7

WHERE IS GOD?

I T IS HARD TO BELIEVE THERE are atheists in this beautiful world of God's grandeur, because everywhere I look I see evidence of God. When we look and really see, and when we hear and really listen, the world becomes filled with miracles that point to our Creator.

So where is God? He is everywhere, just waiting to be found.

I wrote this poem to bear testimony to God's presence and His love for us.

In the wind caressing my face
In a hug and warm embrace

Where Is God?

In the air I breathe
In everything I see
In the wind caressing my face
In a hug and warm embrace
In the blossom budding into bloom
In the quiet and still, alone in a room
In the flowing river, keeper of life
In all creatures living and alive
In beautiful music with notes afloat

In the inspired words poets wrote
In sunsets all orange, red, and pink
In our hearts and minds when we think
In twinkling stars of the dark night
In hundreds of birds taking to flight
In a tender, loving, gentle kiss
In a miracle, a prayer, making a wish
In a newborn baby's first-heard cry
In all the mysteries and reasons why.

Since what may be known about God is plain to them, because God has made it plain to them. For since the creation of the world God's invisible qualities—his eternal power and divine nature—have been clearly seen, being understood from what has been made, so that people are without excuse.

ROMANS 1:19–20

AND THE COWS LAY DOWN

I WAS BLESSED TO HAVE BEEN IN the path of a total solar eclipse. When the eclipse was at its height, there was cloud cover, but I was able to glimpse the moon concealing the sun, and I saw a planet brighten the darkened sky. The birds stopped singing, and the tree frogs began croaking along with the chirping crickets. The cows in the pastures lay down. The temperature noticeably dropped. Crescent shadows were cast, giving an eerie lighting effect.

My mind was taken back to a day long ago when it became dark, the day our Savior died, leaving this world. The saddest day for humanity was also a day of praise and gratitude for His loving sacrifice. He quietly atoned for our sins with His blood. So, looking up to the heavens to view the eclipse, I remembered and gave thanks to God for His Son. This poem came from that experience when the birds became silent and the cows lay down.

*Frozen memories of the
past from a different time
When Heaven cried, when
blackness gave the sign*

And the Cows Lay Down

Darkness came quietly in the middle of the day
Stillness, speechless, no words known to say
Eyes looking up to see starlit celestial skies
Contemplating, Is there some reason why?

Frozen memories of the past from a different time
When Heaven cried, when blackness gave the sign
Never forget, remember, a reminder for us all
The day mankind had its deepest heinous fall

When God Made Man died with one breathless,
* mournful sigh*
Selflessly He left this world to lift us high
"Forgive them, Father," words of His that
* permanently last*

Our future destinies He did dutifully with
* passion cast*

His unspoken pain and sealed tears still remain
For all of us, sinners, He sacrificially came
The Lamb of God, He died to fulfill His love
So, on our knees we give thanks to Him above

For He gave Himself to right all our wrongs
Then the birds ceased singing their songs
And the cows lay down
To honor our Savior on the day we were
* no longer lost, but found*
Amen.

The heavens declare the glory of God; the skies proclaim the work of his hands. Day after day they pour forth speech; night after night they reveal knowledge. They have no speech, they use no words; no sound is heard from them. Yet their voice goes out into all the earth, their words to the ends of the world. In the heavens God has pitched a tent for the sun.

PSALM 19:1–4

THE GIFT OF CHRISTMAS

THERE IS REALLY NO INTRODUCTION TO this poem needed, as Jesus Christ, our beloved Savior, is the true Gift of Christmas, which our merciful God gave to the world because He so loved us. May you feel and know the Gift of Christmas all year long.

Little Child so safely nestled in a curl
You are the Bearer of light given to the world

The Gift of Christmas

The angels came to give You praise
The shepherds stalked to see Your gaze

The Bethlehem star lit up the heavenly sky
To mark earth's gift, life's reason why

The swaddled Babe lay at rest
He has come for us, to do God's best

Mankind He is here to save
No other could be the central nave

He loves with open accepting arms
In them no one can suffer harm

God Made Man for us to live
His life He did so readily give

Little One comes bearing love and truth
Sacrifice and pain is Your final roost

You came to show and lead The Way
Knowing You would lose Your life one day

Loved beyond more than we will ever know
You give us forgiveness so readily to show

Little Child so safely nestled in a curl
You are the Bearer of light given to the world

We, the fallen needy, accept Your grace
Knowing the love given in Your face

You are God's blessing in His sight
You alone will work to make all things right

The Gift of Christmas, our God's delight
Tells the story of His omniscient might

So little heavenly Baby, You sleep tight
While the angels in Heaven celebrate this night

Jesus Christ is The Truth, The Life, and
   The Way
So we give our thanks and praise on this
   Christmas Day.

For to us a child is born, to us a son is given, and the government will be
on his shoulders. And he will be called Wonderful Counselor, Mighty God,
Everlasting Father, Prince of Peace.

ISAIAH 9:6

HE IS RISEN

Not only did Christ take on our sins when He died for us on the cross, He also rose from the dead, conquering death to sit at the right hand of God the Father, who reigns in Heaven. He will come again to reign, on Earth and in Heaven. A mortal man can die, but only the immortal Christ, the Son of God, can rise from the dead on His own accord. Easter Day is our most important religious holiday because it is the crux and foundation of our Christian faith. For He is the Son of God, He is risen, and He lives. So, I write this poem in celebration, proclaiming Jesus Christ, our Savior, the Son of God, has risen on Easter Day!

My eternal life has
not been tossed
Because my Savior died
for me on the cross

He Is Risen

Christ died for me so I might win
He set me free from all my sin
I am innocent as a child once again
Christ is now both my brother and friend

His blood has made me brand-new
It is my heart that He did woo
I saw the light then suddenly knew
My faith and trust in Him then grew

I am now no longer one who is lost
Because of love He paid the cost
My eternal life has not been tossed
Because my Savior died for me on the cross

Always next to me is where Christ stands
He is on my side so I know I will and can
With gratitude and thanks my heart expands
Into His arms is where I rest and land

It comforts me that He is really there
I can bear all, even if the world is unfair
My promise with my life is to always serve
   and care
It is to Him I send my praise and prayers

For Him only my soul longs
Thankfulness lifts my heart to song
My debt is paid, erased, and now gone
Even all my sins, mistakes, and wrongs

For you and me He came to live and die

Then from death on the third day to rise
He is the final answer to all the whys
He paid the price, for my soul He did buy

The Son of God, the Son of man
From the beginning He was part of God's
   eternal plan
He waits for me with His outstretched,
   open hand
Now on my soul I have His seal and brand

God so loved us to give His only Son
It is He who finished it all, now over and done
He calls and beckons for me to come
From Him never again will I ever run

The bondage and shackles have been released
I am now His to always forever keep
My love for God runs strong and deep
Then to Heaven after my final awakened sleep

My Savior He lives on within me
With the Father and Holy Spirit, the Trinity
My soul yearns one day for Him to see
To my heart Christ holds the lasting key

He is the Alpha and Omega, the final say
No longer for my sins do I have to pay
I give glory to God now and will always
Because Christ is risen on Easter Day.

Jesus said to her, "I am the resurrection and the life. The one who believes in me
will live, even though they die."

JOHN 11:25

LOVE'S WELLSPRING

MY MOTHER LIVED TO BE 101 years old. I can say without a doubt that my mother loved me more than anyone on this planet. She loved me with all my imperfections and accepted me as I am.

The unconditional love of a mother is probably the closest thing we have on earth to God's love for us, and it allows us to have a glimpse of how God loves us. If a mother's love is only a glimmer, then just think how much God loves and cares for us. He is where love originates. Love flows from His heart. So, in loving others, we are and remain connected to God.

This poem is dedicated to all the mothers who love their children unconditionally. Thank you for helping us understand the love we receive from God as He loves us despite ourselves. In knowing love, we are also able to love. Love is eternal. God is love.

Love is more than the sum of the parts.
Eternal, enduring, knowing no end—
Love is the wellspring from God's heart.

Love's Wellspring

The unselfish, unconditional love continually
* flows outward and overwhelms me.*
This love is the purest in the world.
It is given with no expectation.
I know the love of God because of you.
To know that I am because of you is enough.
When I feel unworthy, you are there encouraging.
My unsureness vanishes at your touch.
If you are goodness, then I must be the same.
This bond surely cannot break.
Won't I recognize you transformed?
Doesn't the eye know its hand?
Will I know your mother and her mother, too?
It is all connected.
Love is more than the sum of the parts.
Eternal, enduring, knowing no end—
Love is the wellspring from God's heart.

And so we know and rely on the love God has for us. God is love.
Whoever lives in love lives in God, and God in them.

1 JOHN 4:16

TIME TO TIMELESS

TIME HAS ITS BLESSINGS IN THAT it assuages our pain, hurt, sorrow, and loss. It softens thoughts, feelings, and emotions that were formerly intense, at times unbearable or possessive. It also gives us freedom, releasing us from mundane judgments and expectations. But how it is wasted on youth. When we finally discover our true selves, who God created us to be, we find there was much more we could've done with our lives. With this wisdom gained, we then find time conquering and consuming us, hastening us to the finish.

When we are young, time seems to last forever. As we grow older, it starts to contract, almost collapse. It's as if we were accelerating or racing toward the finish line, our true home with God, our Creator. He is our heart's true yearning and longing; only He can fulfill, satisfy, and complete. He gives us endless love.

But love is what
Time can't destroy
It is what brings us real
happiness and joy

Time to Timeless

Time bound by a moment, not clock hands
Our life it holds, controls, and commands
Fleeting as a red bird's song and a
    whip-poor-will's call
Degrading, deteriorating subjects are we all

Vapid vapors vanishing as quickly as they form
As humans Time does mold and conform
A bloom that bursts to just disappear
Death's specter always hovering so very near

Time changes, beings warped by Time
We play and act as mimicking mimes
Once so idle and so lingering
Now, from then hastened, no longer malingering

Time casts memories into the past
Moments gone, lost forever, never to last
So they live only as thoughts in the mind
Not real, imaginary, never to find

But, oh Time, the gift you give to embrace
Softens lost love, pain, and hurt too hard to face
Faded reflected emotions and feelings now lost
When then we thought impossible to bear the cost

Freedom it gives from our old worries and cares
Despite its blessings it remains unfair
Caught and trapped in Time we remain
Outside changing, inside staying the same

We are just muses and jesters, puppetry to the ticking
Time is the master of the foolery and tricking

Where the mind stays still, not joining in
The body becomes aged and worn; it cannot win

The waste on youth is the cruel joke
Then to become lost, empty, no words spoke
Minions to Time, we get left behind
Searching for a reason, but nowhere to find

The past becomes a misty dream, just a blink
An entire lifetime can be contained in God's wink
With Time everything vanishes in the end
Nothing left to hold, to touch, to begin again

All memories fade away
No permanence, never again to stay
But love is what Time can't destroy
It is what brings us real happiness and joy

Built into us is a yearning and longing
We speed up Time toward home for belonging
Love only lasts; it is what was always cast
He loved us first, drawing us to Him so fast

Our lust is for God, our soul's desire
His love is in our hearts, its enduring fire
True love connects us to God above
As He is the origin and source of all love

Timelessness created Time into which we fit
He has woven our life's tapestry with a perfect knit
The sole reason remains and forever is
Our God, who holds the Key; it was always His.

All people are like grass, and all their faithfulness is like the flowers of the field. The grass withers
and the flowers fall, because the breath of the Lord blows on them. Surely the people are grass.
The grass withers and the flowers fall, but the word of our God endures forever.

ISAIAH 40:6–8

A SINNER'S SONG

I WROTE THIS POEM TO EMPHASIZE HOW we sing the same song because we are all sinners in need of redemption. None of us are without sin because God made us perfectly imperfect.

It is only when we as sinners can fall to our knees in surrender and prayer, asking for forgiveness, that God can heal us and make us whole. Then our song can become a song of gratitude, thanks, and praise to God for His loving mercy.

What song are you singing?

I, the wretched sinner,
now have mercy and grace
This is all within the smile of
my sweet Savior's face

A Sinner's Song

I am but a simple sinner just like you
There is no real difference between the two
I can never be perfect as I have flaws
From the beginning of the Fall is the real cause
So I remain a simple sinner no better, no worse
I must live daily bearing this despised curse
A Sinner's Song always ends sadly the same
Because alone I will never win this forsaken game

It is only when I surrender and bow down
To take His bestowed redemptive crown
With hands in the air and knees on the ground
I will no longer be lost, but finally found
I, the wretched sinner, now have mercy and grace
This is all within the smile of my sweet Savior's face
A Sinner's Song is now one of forgiveness and love
It is one of thanks and praise to my Heavenly Father above
Amen.

Whoever conceals their sins does not prosper, but the one
who confesses and renounces them finds mercy.

PROVERBS 28:13

HE

I ORIGINALLY BEGAN THIS POEM WITH MY husband's love for me in mind, but it soon turned into a poem about the One who loves you and me unconditionally, our Lord and Savior. Let us give thanks and praise to God for the birth of His Son, Jesus Christ, who laid His life down so that we may have eternal life.

He lives in my heart, mind, and soul
Walking through dark nights my hand He holds

He

This is the Man I love and who loves me
He loves me even though the real me He sees

Still He has promised to never forsake or leave
By my side in the past, present, and what's to be

He lives in my heart, mind, and soul
Walking through dark nights my hand He holds

He protects and keeps me safe
He watches over me until I wake

He always remains faithful, loving, and kind
No matter what, He remains mine

He makes me into a better person
He is God's Son; of this I am certain

His willing heart is always ready to give
With each breath, it is to serve Him I live

He loves me more than any other
In His wounds for me He suffered

It is only in Him God gives me reprieve
Life without Him I cannot conceive

For Him my heart beats each beat
Each day I thank God that we did meet

It is He I call my Savior and Brother
For me there will never be another

He was born to save me from my sin
It is only through Him that I shall win

He has made the ultimate sacrifice
This He is my beloved, Jesus Christ.

For God so loved the world that he gave his one and only Son, that
whoever believes in him shall not perish but have eternal life.

JOHN 3:16

THE CALL OF THE SEA

THE SEA HAS AN ALLURE THAT beckons us. Its power and might are reminiscent of God's strength. Its tranquility can soothe us with peace, calm, and comfort that can only be from God. This poem is about God's amazing creation, the sea, which mesmerizes and entices us with its beauty and mystery as it gives glory to God. As we look around and really see His creation, we see His great love for us in that He wants us to know who He is.

It has remained unchanged
through all the years
It is constant like God,
who removes all our fears

The Call of the Sea

There is this allure and call of the sea
It has always been throughout the many centuries

As Odysseus heard the sirens' luring song
It reminds us of our origin, for which we long

It's an ancestral legacy, a primordial instinct
Within us, there lies this deep covenant link

Before our breath, in water we lived
It is the sea, to us life it gives

In the beginning the world was covered by the sea
The Holy Spirit hovered over it in stillness
  and mystery

It began a new beginning with Noah in
  biblical history
When God marked His promise with a
  rainbow for us to always see

It allows us to roam the world and be free
As Christ gives us freedom to be you and me

Its salty water is mighty, strong, and can cure
Like God it will also conquer, envelop, and endure

We feel its peace and calm as it gives us rest
Then its destructive powers put our faith to test

The "living water" will remove all God's scorn
In baptism by water we are renewed and reborn

It has remained unchanged through all the years
It is constant like God, who removes all our fears

The sea invites us to join, as does our Creator in
  one unity
This longing is to share with God in loving
  eternal community

✝

Now the earth was formless and empty, darkness was over the surface of the deep,
and the Spirit of God was hovering over the waters.

GENESIS 1:2

PART THREE

Suffering

UNDERSTANDING SUFFERING

I RECEIVED AN EMAIL FROM A WOMAN who had experienced much tragedy in her life and in the lives of her loved ones. She felt that God had led her to my website, where she was able to find some comfort from my personal testimony of the pain and suffering I have experienced in my life and how I have reacted to it. I want to share my response to her as I know so many people struggle with the issue of suffering when there is a loving God. This is the study of theodicy.

We can find joy in knowing God's
love, peace in feeling God's presence,
and hope in believing God's promise.

Dear Friend,

My heart broke hearing your sad story of the pain and suffering you as well as your loved ones have had to experience. There are just some things this side of Heaven that we will never understand in this life. I have written several poems about this. I have come to accept and live with the mystery, believing that God always has our best interest while knowing men are free to make choices that can have dire consequences, but God can redeem this. I think, when I hopefully get to Heaven with my list of questions, I will arrive and will just know the answers, discarding my list. I also believe God is merciful and knows our true hearts. We certainly can't hide anything from Him. I trust that He knows how mental illness and deep pain can cause people to commit suicide and do things that are not true reflections of who they are. I also believe that there is never a sin too big that God cannot forgive if we come with a repentant heart. I have chosen to continue to trust God and believe He is pure love. Ultimately, we must make a choice in how to live our lives, knowing that bad things will happen in this life because of free choice and random occurrences. In choosing to live life with our cups half full, not half empty, we can be confident that God can fill our cups even to overflowing. He can redeem, restore, rebuild, and heal our brokenness. There is always hope, and He can bring good from even the worst circumstance for those who love Him. Nothing, absolutely nothing, is impossible with God. So, ultimately, we must walk by faith, not by what we see and experience. I wish I could remove all the pain and suffering I as well as my loved ones have experienced, but we live in a fallen world. We have never been promised a life free of pain, but God has promised He will never forsake us or abandon us, remaining with us and suffering with us. Our hope remains in God's promise knowing there is eternal life with our rewards found in the glory of Heaven, where there is no longer pain and suffering. Our faith and belief are something that no one on this planet can take from us. So, we can find joy in knowing God's love, peace in feeling God's presence, and hope in believing God's promise. May you know God's love, feel His presence, and believe His promise always.

Love and blessings to you and yours,
Rhonda

As I was with Moses, so I will be with you; I will never leave you nor forsake you. . . .
Have I not commanded you? Be strong and courageous. Do not be afraid; do not be
discouraged, for the Lord your God will be with you wherever you go.

JOSHUA 1:5, 9

SORROW TO SONG

I WROTE THIS POEM ABOUT EXPERIENCING DEEP loss as I did with the death of my twenty-five-year-old son in April 2011. This can be any loss that causes great suffering. Sometimes the loss is due to a poor decision or maybe an accident. Over the years, the stinging pain lessens, but it always remains. But, as I carry this pain, I can also experience great joy simultaneously. Sorrow can become a song when God keeps His promise of Romans 8:28. He can transform the worst tragedy and bring good from it for those who love Him and are called to serve Him.

My sorrow still lives and will live on
But now my heart also sings a joyful song

Sorrow to Song

I carry such deep sorrow
It will never end with tomorrow

I have learned to live with the pain
I do not look for any change or gain

Choices have left their mark
They remain closely nestled in the dark

Any distraction from the constant ache
Shadows of hurt looming are my mistake

A moment's joy of laughter gives reprieve
But never can it fulfill my heart's inner need

If I could only grasp to take my leave
I wish my mind could hope and conceive

The torn hole still lives within
It festers with knowledge of my sin

So I carry my sorrow, the sadness lives
I am trapped, not knowing where and
   what to give

Help me, Lord, my heart to unlock
If only I could turn back once more the clock

Happiness will never now be truly mine
But I will manage to cope, somehow be fine

The discontent is now solid and bound
No solace or relief will ever be found

Searing loss has been the cost
My heart now seems permanently lost

I can't repair; the damage is done
Even pretending, ignoring, playing at fun

A moment's escape releases my trap
But no changing or breaking the lethal mishap

So my cross to bear I will carry my burden
My heart goes on, it will grow and burgeon

Sacrifice is my lasting, sacramental device
This is enough, it must and will suffice

In my brokenness, I am Yours to fully serve
Wounded healer, my name is deserved

Please, God, lift this pain
Don't let me continue to stay the same

Use my suffering to make some good
Yes, heal me, Lord, if only somehow You could

God, You can make things right
When I walk by faith, not by sight

Turning to You, I wish I had
With You I can hold both, joy and sad

With You all things are made possible today
It is You who knows and leads the Way

Only You can make me again whole
My life You transform and mold

My sorrow still lives and will live on
But now my heart also sings a joyful song

And we know that in all things God works for the good of those
who love him, who have been called according to his purpose.

ROMANS 8:28

THE WAY BACK

SOMETIMES WE INADVERTENTLY GET LOST. WE lose our way. We stray from God, turning away from Him. We choose to indulge our own wants and desires for short-lived gratification. We stray off course and may find we don't know the way back.

I wrote this poem to acknowledge how, in our humanness, we can easily slip and find ourselves lost. But the way back is always present when we turn with intentionality toward God with repentance and prayer. We can find our way back with God's help.

Repentance is the
first step taken
Otherwise our souls
will be lost, forsaken

The Way Back

Sometimes we get lost and need to find
    the way back
Somehow or other we have gone off track
It can happen so quick, so very fast
If not careful it may persist, always last

A few slips, small white lies
Can have us asking ourselves why
Maybe things we failed to mention
But we didn't have any real intention

Daily surrenders, little mistakes
Move us from God, keep us awake
We say just the mind's idea with no action
They can persist, sin by a mere fraction

Desires, covets, passions, wants
These are not innocent, simple thoughts
They take us off our straight course and path
Our grim fate may then be forever cast

Looming temptation specters may lead us
    into a dark shadow
For the way into the Light is not broad,
    but narrow
Behaviors are derived from emotions
    and feelings
Reflections of our hearts, our true beings

How to climb out of this deep dark hole
Before our hearts it forever molds
Repentance is the first step taken
Otherwise our souls will be lost, forsaken

To the ground on our knees looking up
Prayer is what does and can interrupt
Forgiveness from God will make us whole
Preventing sin from taking its complete hold

Conversations and time with God
    are needed
To His plan we must be fully conceded
Intentionality with effort to do His will
Practice and practice to hone this skill

We need His help, His love, His strength
Be committed to go the complete length
We cannot do this by ourselves alone
He will see our souls when we stand
    before His throne

But our God is for us, not against us
Believe this to our core, we must
Put Him first, above everything and all
Then we can find our way back, hearing
    His call.

If I rise on the wings of the dawn, if I settle on the far side of the sea, even
there your hand will guide me, your right hand will hold me fast.

PSALM 139:9–10

INTO THE LIGHT

EVERY DAY WE DEAL WITH HUNDREDS of choices. Sometimes we are not consciously aware of what we think, speak, and do. We are constantly choosing light or darkness, good or evil, right or wrong. Small surrenders of seemingly no significant outcome can gradually accumulate, pushing us down that slippery slope to sin. Soon we find ourselves surrounded by darkness. We are either turning toward God or away from Him. It is only He who can lead us from the dark into the light.

Into our darkness God will shine His light
When we decide to walk by faith and not by sight

Into the Light

Dark shadows we shed may stay and linger
Within our souls they can persist and malinger

The flesh and the world are two contentious strongholds
Our character and future they can permanently
change and mold

Repeated sinful thoughts may fester and manifest
It is Satan who is present, putting us to the test

Small surrenders can permanently last
Added together our future they may cast

Resisting temptation will give the human spirit
no rest
God will help us, but we must pray and request

It is only He who can shine a light for our feet
To show us the way so we won't suffer permanent defeat

God does not want us to lose, He is on our side
But within our hearts there is nothing from Him
we can hide

The choice of light or dark we each must make
Every moment we choose so don't forsake

One day unknown our demise we will meet
Our choices determine who will be there to greet

Each former decision can bear its heavy weight
Deathbed remorse and wishes may be made too late

Into the light, the only way for an eternal
heavenly fate
On our own without God's grace we will never rate

Into our darkness God will shine His light
When we decide to walk by faith and not by sight.

Your word is a lamp for my feet, a light on my path.

PSALM 119:105

IF I CAN JUST KEEP
ON BREATHING

GLOOMY WINTER DAYS CAN BE A time of year when some can fall into a depression. This may lead to despair and feelings of hopelessness.

I lost my twenty-five-year-old son to shallow-water blackout while he was practicing breath-holding in our pool; I almost lost my oldest daughter to heroin addiction; I also nearly lost my youngest daughter because of her three-month premature birth. My husband has suffered from cancer; I lost my father to cancer; my mother had Alzheimer's disease. I personally know my own human frailties, deep loss, heartbreak, despair, and hopelessness—a brokenness unspoken. But I found if I could just focus on the right thing, if I could just keep on breathing, I could make my way to the next day that held hope.

So never ever give up the faith that a new day can bring promise of relief. Ceasing breathing is never the answer; it is always the permanent solution to a temporary problem. No matter how bad it seems, it will always get better if you can just keep on breathing . . . and believing.

I am an admitted wounded and broken healer. It is that brokenness, those cracks within us, that lets God into our hearts to bring healing and hope.

My heart has been torn from me once again
There is nowhere to go, to try to begin

If I Can Just Keep On Breathing

What do you do when you are broken and alone?
When there is no one to tell or even phone?

Where do you go with all your pain
When you are the only one left to blame?

This brokenness cannot be spoken
Only heartbreak and suffering are the token

All I can see is that it is the end
There is nothing left to darn, nothing left to mend

My heart has been torn from me once again
There is nowhere to go, to try to begin

So death seems so easy, a place for my hope
I have lost all ability to live and to cope

If I can just keep breathing for one more day
Surely God will help me find my way

The fear and abandonment keep closing in
All thoughts are consumed; this must be the end

The pain rips through to my core
My heart will cease if the hurt becomes any more

Please don't leave me alone; don't go away
I can't bear the hurt; please ask me to stay

The lost tears of deep desperation and despair
Know this heart is broken with no hope of repair

The solitary control left
Is to meet with surly death

My consolation is the grave
So I must try to be brave

My mind tells me there is no other way
Unless my life remains in an isolated cave

Destiny does not follow the planned course
Every cell in my body feels the remorse

When desolation and desecration are mine
There is only a barren void that I am able to find

The empty abyss welcomes with open arms
I am not afraid; I fear no more harm

If all are better without me
Darkness shed is the shadow I see

Left alone for eternity, embracing loneliness
My punishment is this, but please, one last kiss

The moment passes as an unknown lifetime
The searing cut of forgiveness is my only lifeline

If I can just keep breathing for one more day
Surely God can help me find my way

I pray my brokenness will go away
I pray my heart will want me to stay

The sun rises, bringing the contemplation of hope
God is giving me prayers, helping me to cope

This brokenness He can only heal
He knows my heart and how I feel

The deep hole I find myself in
Allows me to see God once again

I can only look up to see His face
That is when I am bathed by His loving grace

So my hope and promise alone are in Him
Sadness looms near, but never again

If I can just keep breathing for one more day
Surely God will show me the way

Brokenness can be healed by faith and belief
The Lord God, my Savior, is the only relief

If I can just keep breathing for one more day
I know God will show me the way.

Therefore, there is now no condemnation for those who are in Christ Jesus,
because through Christ Jesus the law of the Spirit who gives life has set you free
from the law of sin and death. . . . In all these things we are more than conquer-
ors through him who loved us.

Romans 8:1–2, 37

I STUMBLE AND FALL DOWN

PAUL'S STRUGGLE WITH SIN DESCRIBED IN Romans 7 resonates within me. It is an enigma to me why I sin when I don't want to, yet I still do. There is always a battle of some kind within us. We each have our own special vulnerabilities that make us weak and susceptible to sin. Being aware of one's own weaknesses keeps us guarded and protected. Even so, I find myself stumbling and falling down . . . again and again.

His mercy and grace are extended to me
He helps me once again to clearly see

I Stumble and Fall Down

I stumble and fall down
But Jesus helps me off the ground

Just when I think life is good
Standing the best I could

Then I fall into my own hole dug
I regret again with "shoulds" and "woulds"

It's my blame; it's always the same
My wants and desires, the human hunger game

The person I see in the mirror taunts
My mistakes, wrongs, and errors constantly haunt

Why do I do what I do
When I know I knew what I knew

How can I stoop and bend that low
Continually knocking myself with each blow

In my dark hole, it is lonely and cold
The falling over and over will take its toll

The battle rages, living within
As I struggle and joust with my very own sin

Sometimes I have no idea where to begin
And I think the torment will never end

How do I find my way out
From my hole I scream, cry, and shout

Nowhere to go, the darkness blinds my sight
It seems each time, I just can't get it right

So nowhere to look but up to the Light
To see God staring into my sight

His mercy and grace are extended to me
He helps me once again to clearly see

So I stumbled and fell down
But Jesus was there to help me back off
the ground.

I do not understand what I do. For what I want to do I do not do, but what I hate I do. . . . As it is, it is no longer I myself who do it, but it is sin living in me. For I know that good itself does not dwell in me, that is, in my sinful nature. For I have the desire to do what is good, but I cannot carry it out. For I do not do the good I want to do, but the evil I do not want to do—this I keep on doing. Now if I do what I do not want to do, it is no longer I who do it, but it is sin living in me that does it. . . . What a wretched man I am! Who will rescue me from this body that is subject to death? Thanks be to God, who delivers me through Jesus Christ our Lord!

ROMANS 7:15, 17–20, 24–25

DO YOU REALLY SEE ME?

A S A THERAPIST, I DEAL WITH mental illness, and I see the suffering it inflicts. Our mental health-care system has failed those it was meant to serve and help, turning many onto the streets homeless with no care. This plight of those with mental illness has touched my heart deeply so I have written a poem from their perspective about what they face daily and how they are treated. The second commandment is not just to love others as you would want to be loved, but in John 15:12 we are told to love others as Jesus would love them. This is a much greater command and something we must all search our hearts and be accountable for. How those with mental challenges are treated is also our responsibility, because we are called to love our brothers and sisters.

I pray every morning
always each day
Hoping God will guide
me down the right way

My command is this: Love each other as I have loved you.

JOHN 15:12

Do You Really See Me?

Do you really see me and my soul?
Then you would know your disdain and rejection
  have taken their toll

I can look normal on the outside like you or anyone
But inside racing thoughts are always on the run

Sometimes my expressions may not seem quite right
As worry and anxiety cause my reactions to be
  freeze, fight, or flight

I do not mean to cause anyone harm
But I see in your face such fear and alarm

Sometimes reality I just cannot conceive
Which may cause me to suddenly respond or
  abruptly leave

I know I am difficult to understand and perceive
When it is only sensitivity and love that I
  desperately need

I may act strange and react with emotion
Though I never mean to cause and provoke
  such commotion

Time flees by without meaning or reason
My erratic moods can change season to season

I wish I could be reliable and plan
But these things, it seems, I never can

Demons in my mind go freely to and fro
I have no control; I can never know

As hard as I try I can't be what you want
The ridicule, disappointment, and hurt
  persistently taunt

I have embarrassed my family so they shun me
If they only knew my heart then they would see

I have no place to call my own home
So in the streets I continually and aimlessly roam

On the roads I wander and have no rest
I forage and scavenge, working my best

Soundless tears drip from my tired, worn face
As I plead for anyone, a stranger, to hear my needy case

My loneliness is a hidden shroud from within
My isolation and oddity are not a vagrant's sin

But I do adore my Jesus with all my heart
He loves me, even if from others I remain apart

I am still God's child just like you
My compassion is real and sincere if only you knew

So look at me with kindness and sympathy
I need your mercy, love, and empathy

I am not a criminal; I don't belong in jail
If only someone would just listen to my sad, lonely tale

My life just needs someone to care and constancy
My hope is for more humanity and honesty

I try so hard, but continually fail
I persist and pursue, but to no avail

I pray every morning always each day
Hoping God will guide me down the right way

Darkness hangs over me like a black cloud
I have nowhere to go; I am not allowed

I need your love, someone to help me now
But will you find aid for me, someway, somehow

If you could really see me
As Jesus knows and sees

It would be my saving hope, my future's life key
I then could find the peace of God and finally just live to be

So please, dear friend, don't ever lose sight
Don't forget those like me that daily fight
A difficult battle and challenging plight.

NO ONE KNOWS

I DON'T EVEN REMEMBER THE CIRCUMSTANCE, AS it was many years ago, but I was having a bad day. It seemed to me that my family might be better off without me. I was driving down the road when a fleeting thought passed through my mind: It would be so easy to just drive into that big tree and all my pain and suffering would end. Well, the thought passed and I didn't act on it. I am not suicidal and never really was. But my point is that if I have had this passing thought, then I know that many have and that many are even contemplating suicide at this moment.

I was in church and the guest minister was speaking about suicide. He called to the altar all those who were considering suicide as a solution. I was astounded at the number who went forward, especially the proportion of young people.

To all of you who are thinking that suicide is the answer to your problems, I am saying it's not. The answer is reaching out to others for help and looking up from the bottom of the dark hole you are in to see God, who is waiting to help you. You are never alone. Suicide is never the solution.

So you reach out into the dark
night to find His hand
With trust you know by your side
He will forever stand

No One Knows

You see me on the outside, but no one knows
Others think everything is fine, but you know
  it isn't so
The suffering within, those unseen tears
Secret thoughts you have hidden for years

Afraid, isolated, feeling all alone
Never having a safe place to feel at home
No person you think can ever understand
They don't know, but you have an escape plan

You keep trying so hard each and every day
Looking and searching to find your way
From the bottomless pit you see no glimmer of light
It seems easier and easier to give up the fight

Passing refrains, mind echoes, whispers of suicide
You wish those words of the solution were untrue,
  all lies
But the suffering, the darkness, the lingering pain
It all seems to be pushing you, driving you closer
  to insane

There is something lacking, something gone amiss
Life is unhinged, it's too great a risk
The increasing layers on layers of pain hurts
  your heart

Trying to pretend otherwise makes it all a farce
You are tired of persisting; you don't want to live
  any longer
You pray to God you wish you were stronger
All these spectrally thoughts you know are wrong
With no hope, you are approaching your final song

You plead for just a small wisp of hope
Something to cling to, for your mind to cope
Anything to release this deadly grip of despair
Finally, you accept that life is just always unfair

But His promise is to not leave, to not forsake
Can you just have the patience to persist and wait?
Someway, somehow God can make it all right
When you can finally walk by faith, not by sight

So you reach out into the dark night to find
  His hand
With trust you know by your side He will
  forever stand
You bask in His eternal love, strength, and care
Now, there is no pain too great for you to bear.

✝

For God, who said, "Let light shine out of darkness," made his light shine in our
hearts to give us the light of the knowledge of God's glory displayed in the face of
Jesus Christ.

2 CORINTHIANS 4:6

WHEN YOU DON'T UNDERSTAND

MY HEART KEEPS ON BREAKING. I see and feel so much pain, sadness, and suffering. There is so much that we just don't understand, and we may never understand, in this life. Lord, be with us through these trials and tribulations.

Your heart is crushed, torn, and broken
So many words have been left unspoken

When You Don't Understand

When life makes no sense and you don't
  understand the reason why
Your life unravels before your very eyes

You look to find an answer somewhere
You look to find something, someone to
  help and care

Your heart is crushed, torn, and broken
So many words have been left unspoken

The tears roll out from a hidden, deep place
The hurt and heartbreak show all over your face

Life seems unbearable with shame and disgrace
You look to find shelter, but there is no place

The hurt is too much to try to carry on
Your heartstrings are cut, losing their song

Is it possible to still make your way?
Can you go on breathing for another day?

You think your heart will stop, will miss its
  next beat
The dark specter lurks near, waiting to leap

Cold, still sleep seems to be the only answer
Fear and sadness have become your cancer

You question if you are going insane
You don't know how to play this heart game

There is nowhere left to go
Never have you felt so very, very low

You don't understand the reason or cause for such hurt
You wish there was someone to help and alert

The sadness looms and does not go away
Speaking is useless, there is nothing left to say
When the cruel words are like a viper's sting
The pain still echoes with a continuous ring

You feel like a broken and wounded bird
You only want your hurt and sorrow to be
  acknowledged and heard

Who is there to turn to, but only God
But only stillness and silence, there is no nod

Sometimes no response can give you grace
Unanswered prayers may be the case

You scream and cry out with all your might
Please, dear God, help make things right

You won't give in, give up the fight
Your faith in Him will never lose its sight

In unexplained mystery you must rest
God's help and His strength are still your quest

He will be found because you seek
Blessed are the suffering, not just the meek

You will continue your trust and your belief
Even if Heaven will be your only relief

Your faith in God alone, you will always keep
What is sown on earth, in Heaven you will reap.

Therefore we do not lose heart. . . . For our light and momentary troubles are achiev-
ing for us an eternal glory that far outweighs them all.

2 CORINTHIANS 4:16, 17

LIVING IN THE VALLEYS OF LIFE

HOW DO WE LIVE DAY AFTER day when we can't seem to get out of the valley?

Take a deep breath. Feel the stress, fear, worry, anxiety, and panic release from your body. Then sit in acceptance, being aware of exactly where you are. Notice as your feelings begin to change, lessen, and assuage.

As we begin to rest and observe our surroundings, we might find that in the valley there is grass, maybe green pastures, to nourish and help us grow. Valleys are lush and green with life because there is usually a stream flowing through to refresh and restore with the waters of life. If we keep looking and seeking, we will see the Shepherd tending His flock with love and care and protecting them. We will find that His rod and staff will give us the comfort of His constant presence. It is He alone who will lead us out of the valley, guiding us along the safe path up to the mountaintop. When we look back down to the valley, we will then see just how far we have come.

It is He alone who will lead us out of the Valley, guiding us along the safe path up to the mountaintop.

The Lord is my shepherd, I lack nothing. He makes me lie down in green pastures, he leads me beside quiet waters, he refreshes my soul. He guides me along the right paths for his name's sake. Even though I walk through the darkest valley, I will fear no evil, for you are with me: your rod and your staff, they comfort me.

PSALM 23:1–4

YOU CAME WITH ANGEL'S WINGS

I F YOU HAVE EVER LOVED A special dog and felt the unconditional love and acceptance that was given to you, then you know dogs are God's four-legged angels on earth. This poem is dedicated to them—too many to name. Thank you for bringing such joy and comfort into our lives. And that goes for those special cats, too.

All dogs go to Heaven; there is no choice
So little doggy angels, together we rejoice

You Came with Angel's Wings

You came into my life with angel's wings
Bringing me joy, lifting my heart up to sing

I remember the adoring eyes and snaggletooth face
I long for one more lick, one more embrace

Your love filled me up, again and again
Now I've lost my very best friend

Just to feel one last wet, tender kiss
Your love and devotion I will always miss

True unconditional love I do now know
Little one so dear, I miss and loved you so

You always could comfort and relieve my fears
So now I sit crying, shedding my streaming tears

Your blind, undying love is like no other
It even rivals the love of a devoted mother

My heart you left is now with a hole
That can only be filled by your sweet little soul

You lived each one of your days to please
My loneliness you were always able to fill and ease

You stole my heart only then to break it
Without you in my life it will be hard to make it

Oh, how I miss your wagging tail
With your endless love I could never fail

Without your love I feel such sorrow
I cannot imagine my empty tomorrow

For me you would sacrifice your life
For me you would take on any strife

The loss I feel is so deep and real
I pray to God to someway help me heal

You pulled my heartstrings then they tangle
This is real love no matter the angle

How can I get through this pain?
Because of one little pup, I will never be the same

God sent you to be His comforter, for us you care
So I will open my heart again, it is worth the price
and the fare

It is to know this special kind of love
To be sure it is from God up above

It will be hard, but I will try again
Risking my heart to lose my best friend

Your short number of years will have to suffice
As all your love gave me such an enriched life

So my little earth angel, take your flight
You are Heaven bound after the sleepy night

I know that God holds your special place
Then one day we will see each other face-to-face

All dogs go to Heaven; there is no choice
So little doggy angels, together we rejoice

We will then run, frolic, and play
We will be together again on that happy day

So they come to earth with cold, wet noses and
angel's wings to say
It is God who has made it all this way

So no wonder it is not odd
That "dog" spelled backward is "God."

Blessed are the meek, for they will inherit the earth.

MATTHEW 5:5

THE LONG GOODBYE

MY MOTHER DIED FROM DEMENTIA. I have written this poem that addresses bearing witness to slow, terminal diseases such as Alzheimer's and how hard it is to see your loved one vanish painfully before your eyes, knowing they would never choose this for themselves. The end of the poem raises the question: How far does love and benevolence go? What would God want and how would He judge? These are difficult questions that we must struggle with as a society, culture, and world. What is really right or wrong or merciful? I leave that up to you to answer.

What would you want if it were you experiencing the long goodbye?

I lost my dear mother over a period of more than ten years. My only comfort was seeing her well cared for and in no apparent pain. She never would have wanted her life to end as it did. I pray she did not suffer. I observed a few grimaces as she neared death, so I suspect she was not totally pain-free, even though she was on pain medication. This long goodbye has made me consider the difficulty of this experience for our loved ones and us. This poem, "The Long Goodbye," arises from the feelings and contemplations experienced when losing a loved one over a long period of time.

One moment a glimpse of who they are
Then they are gone somewhere so far

The Long Goodbye

The long goodbye will bring tears to your eyes
The relationship vanishes, disappears, and
  finally dies

As you slowly, painfully lose the person
Life becomes unknown and uncertain

The empty body is still there
You cry out to God with anger; it's not fair

The living dead is what's seen and said
You live in fear, facing the future with dread

The person you love is being slowly erased
These trials and tribulations are too difficult
  to face

Their smiles, their laughter, the glimmer in
  their eyes
Gone and wasting away, it makes you cry

One moment a glimpse of who they are
Then they are gone somewhere so far

Your heart is barren and lonely, but still cares
Your mind wanders to reality, and you feel
  so scared

The human connection is now long gone
You proclaim this is not right, so very wrong

You touch their skin, still warm as they stare
  into space
Blank and forlorn is the look on their face

Can they just slip away and stay with no pain?
Close their eyes then in permanent sleep remain

Someway, somehow, this is God's plan, you trust
These thoughts you claim, you believe, you must

One final last lingering forever kiss
To the one you love, will always miss

Sadly with resign, you walk away slowly, closing
  the door
The suffering is gone; the pain will be no more.

He will wipe every tear from their eyes. There will be no more death or mourning
or crying or pain, for the old order of things has passed away.

REVELATION 21:4

WHEN IT'S OVER

WITH THE LOSS OF MY MOTHER and my son, watching friends with life-threatening illnesses, and the loss of individuals daily around the world, impending death always remains near, on my mind and heart. These thoughts have led me to write the poem "When It's Over." I actually first shared this poem at my beloved mother's memorial service, as it was inspired by her death.

Experiencing a deep loss with no explainable cause
Gives you a reason to think and pause

When It's Over

What do you do when it's over?
When there is no place or time to start over?

You see your life coming to an end
There is no chance to begin again

What will really last
As your life sped by so fast?

They say it's what's within your dash
It's the love given out, not the cash

How many lives have been touched and changed?
It's the lasting effect for the long range

If you had a chance to redo
Would you see life's meaning and its clues?

We are all the small creatures scratching symbols on
our walls
Never contemplating our future falls

Each breath taken could founder past
So it matters all the chosen players in your cast

Each day should be sung as your last song
Using the time to try and right all your wrongs
You don't know the number of your days
Life is about caring and compassion in so
many ways

Experiencing a deep loss with no explainable cause
Gives you a reason to think and pause

Reflecting on the significance and meaning
Gives credence to our humanity and being

What is life's purpose, you say?
The answer is there when you find your way

A life lived of love is everything
In Heaven and on earth it reigns

All those painful and joyous tears lost
and shed
Were meant to bring you life's knowledge before you
were dead

So turn inside and within to feel your heart
That is when you will finally become smart

See all the miracles surrounding you to see
Dream and dream big as to what could be

Each of us has our own journey and tale
Always rise up, never be afraid to fall or fail

So what's on your future epitaph
That will endure and really last?

Wonder if you will have to account
Things done and not done to recount

Kindness, love, and mercy to all
These are thoughts and memories to recall

Fate may not allow you to wait
One moment to the next, you may be at
Heaven's gate

What will you say?
What will you have to pay?

Wondering when it's all over

What will be next in the order?

*Things to ponder and consider before it's
  too late*
Before you meet your own fateful date

You always have another chance
Until you dance your final dance

What will be your fate?
How will you rate?

*How will you be remembered when it's
  all done?*
*What will you say when you come
  face-to-face with the Son?*

*So what will be said with your one
  last breath?*
Will there be no sadness or regret?

When the final curtain falls
How do you think God will judge it all?

Teach us to number our days, that we may gain a heart of wisdom.

PSALM 90:12

A REFLECTION ON THE DEATH OF MY SON:

A LAMENT OF PROMISE

Gene Whitner Milner III
December 10, 1985 to April 17, 2011

My son died on Palm Sunday at 7:30 p.m. I went out to our pool to turn off the cabana lights. That is when I discovered my beautiful twenty-five-year-old son on the bottom of the pool. My nightmare had begun, as the worst thing possible had just happened to me, the untimely death of one of my children. I remember feeling it was surreal as I observed myself from outside my body. Looking at a desperate, panic-stricken woman, not knowing what to do, until she let out a scream, a deep primitive guttural cry of defiance to Death and God.

Well, I have lived and breathed through the pain and survived. Some say we reach and adjust to a new "normal," but I will never be normal again. What I have found is a new reality. We never get over grief, but we do get used to living with it. Ideally, it becomes integrated into us as part of who we are, but not our identity. Several years later, I went to Sedona, Arizona, to become a Compassionate Bereavement Care™ provider with Dr. Joanne Cacciatore. This is part of my healing—to walk beside others as they grieve and mourn, being a loving and compassionate presence. The fact alone that I am alive and functioning, enjoying life while I still hold deep inner sorrow is enough to give others hope.

I would never wish this tragedy on anyone, and I certainly wish it had never happened to me, but I can say I am glad that I am the person I am today compared to how I was before my loss. I often think of a gardener who prunes bushes with deep cuts to stimulate new growth and make the plant healthier and stronger. Pain has a way of growing you into a better, more compassionate, caring, and sensitive person with perspective on what is most important in life. That can be summed up with one word—*love*.

I know if my son had a chance to come back he would not because he has already crossed God's finish line well. I know with confidence we will meet again one day face-to-face. Until then, I will serve God with all the experiences and gifts that He has given me, so maybe on my last day I will hear the words we all long for:

Well done, good and faithful servant!

MATTHEW 25:21

I wrote this sorrowful lament after my son died in response to the deep pain of grief and loss I felt. It does end with hope on the horizon, hence the title, "A Lament of Promise." I pray my words bring some comfort to anyone who has suffered the loss of a loved one.

My son died from underwater breath-holding in our pool, succumbing to shallow water blackout. My family has founded a nonprofit to raise awareness and educate in hopes of stopping these senseless, preventable deaths.

Please see www.shallowwaterblackoutprevention.org to understand the dangers of breath-holding underwater.

From sorrow may spring a joyful song
A secret silver lining may be submerged
within the sadness

A Lament of Promise

My broken heart goes on beating.
My breath is not ceasing.
The sadness looms and hovers near—
a dash away, a moment's fear.

The shadow creeps from within
arising in the emptiness
where you once were but dwell no more.

The memories languish-laced
in my passing thoughts
echoing through my mind.

Timelessness hangs with me
swinging on the moment
where I think you still exist.

The dewy mist fills my eyes
with saltless tears of sorrow
emerging from the heart's deepest chamber.

A look, a face, a warm embrace
brings the remembrance of what once was,
but never now to be.

There is consolation
found in the touch and image of a hazy,
  foggy dream,
though that vision fades as a vapor
lost to the dawn's faint light and a
  red bird's call.

I wait for our unanticipated meeting again,
not to be missed—
my heart pines with longing
and yearns for days gone missing.

Muffled cries with liquid prayers
mourn in quiet desperation
surrounded by the black cloak of darkness.

The quiver of morning glimmers
to give a glimpse of hope
to find only a soft whisper.

But, from sorrow
may spring a joyful song.

A secret silver lining
may be submerged within the sadness.

Only You can transform
to the new birth
of a different time.

A separate reality
on the crimson horizon
rises from the dust of ashes
to a new day.

It is a mystery.

At last, a lament of promise lingers,
patiently to be awakened
and to be known.

Blessed are those who mourn, for they will be comforted.

MATTHEW 5:4

THE LANGUAGE OF LOSS

S O MANY OF US HAVE SUFFERED the pain and heartbreak of deep loss. We are actually victims since we did not cause or even anticipate our loss. We venture into a new territory of feelings and emotions that have never been experienced. We learn a new language; it is the language of loss.

He can hold you up by
grasping your hand
With Him by your side,
you know you can

The Language of Loss

When you experience deep loss
You learn a new language, but you pay the cost
Words that had no meaning before
Now you cannot hide from or ignore
Searing hurt and guttural pain
Unasked knowledge is the brutal gain

Never again to be the former or same
Only permanent, lasting change remains
No second chance, no replay, no going back
Your prior world is lost, has gone off track
A new, unexpected fate has been set and cast
This is the unforeseen future that will now
   always last

New words linger, fester, and torment the mind
Looking and searching, but no cure to find
Thoughts streaming with no logic or control
Trying to discover your new identity and role
A different, foreign reality has been discovered
You pray and wish it was some other

Into your broken heart a lasting scar is torn
An indelible badge branded now worn
Sadness and suffering are your close friends
Desolation and depression are new kin
Longing for something that now can't be
Things desired and wants never to see

How to survive and keep on going
Trying to find your way, but not knowing
Burdens so hard and painful to bear
You wish your heart did not ache, did not care
This journey uncharted, destination unknown
But one you must maneuver and venture alone

To survive, God's promises are the sole answers
   and hope
Language of loss, only He can help you to cope
He can hold you up by grasping your hand
With Him by your side, you know you can
Quietly listening for His still small voice
God will lead the way if you make the choice.

For I am convinced that neither death nor life, neither angels nor demons, neither the
present nor the future, nor any powers, neither height nor depth, nor anything else in all
creation, will be able to separate us from the love of God that is in Christ Jesus our Lord.

ROMANS 8:38–39

CHOICES

"CHOICES" WAS WRITTEN TO REFLECT ON the magnitude of consequences our decisions can determine. A zealot runs a car into an innocent crowd or ties a bomb to himself, killing unsuspecting children. An act of harmless flirting quickly turns into a devastating affair, destroying families. Cheating or stealing just once only to get caught with punitive results, little white lies that blow up into violations of trust and destroy relationships, or a decision to drink and drive accidentally takes another's life—all the results of what we choose to do. We make a series of choices every day that can lead us into sin and darkness. The choices we make can shape our future and final fate.

God grants us freedom to decide
To be with Him or not, our final
destiny to bide

Choices

All choices must be made with diligent care
As results, outcomes, consequences can be
  so unfair

A negligent accident, a pulled trigger, a lit bomb,
All are consequences shaping who we become

A smile, a nod, a small sacrifice
Can end up being more than just nice

A stone dropped into a pond
The ripple effect goes on and on and beyond

Choices are free to choose
But not to determine what comes due

A leap of faith, it must take
To one day see our Maker's face

Too busy, too tired, do it later, we say
Then we find out we have lost our way

Life becomes a series of choices
Even with silence, not using our voices

Sometimes we must make a firm,
  unwavering stand
It can determine on which side of the fence
  we land

Our outstretched, compassionate, helping hands
Can keep us from sinking into a void
  of quicksand

We are held accountable for every mistake
We never know when and if it may be too late

Death will come ringing, we don't make
  the date
With each second, we may have cast our fate

All these choices remain up to us
So think with cognitive intention we must

God grants us freedom to decide
To be with Him or not, our final destiny to bide.

✝

If any of you lacks wisdom, you should ask God, who gives generously to all
without finding fault, and it will be given to you.

JAMES 1:5

BETRAYAL

I AM OFTEN ASKED TO ADDRESS DATING and marriage relationships. I believe the most destructive issue that these relationships can face is a betrayal. This poem is about the betrayed and the betrayer. Betrayal in relationships can damage us to the core. Often, there can be no repair or healing. The only healthy way a couple can survive is with God at the center of their relationship. A two-legged stool cannot stand, but a three-legged stool can stand strong without falling. When we look to God and grow closer to Him, we grow closer to each other as a couple. God then becomes the healing presence.

For love to persist after betrayal, pride must give way to humility. Humility prevents shaming of the other party. You see, guilt keeps one from repeating a harmful act, but shame damages. When remorse and amends are greeted with mercy and forgiveness, there can be restitution and restoration of love in a relationship. Though this type of restitution might seem impossible for people, it is not impossible with God. Therefore, we turn to Him for our strength and fortitude to keep love alive.

I wrote the poem "Betrayal" with these thoughts in mind.

The searing brand
remains on a lost heart
Wounds, scars, hurt from
going too far

Betrayal

To know the hurt and the pain
The feeling of going and staying insane

Actors of charades on both sides
Living and breathing in the shadows of disguise
Fearing discovery will be the cause of permanent demise

The searing brand remains on a lost heart
Wounds, scars, hurt from going too far

Picking or choosing can destroy both sides
Severed promises covered by loathsome lies
Must now be willing to say forever goodbyes

Lessons learned, but way too late
Lasting actions can seal the future's fate

Hearts left scattered and all broken
Lust and desire were the mere tokens
So many thoughts, words left unspoken

Souls once bound then forever torn
Enduring coffins sealed with scorn

Too many traumatic bridges left to mend
Trying and trying, but all pretend
It seems impossible, no one can win

The torture and memories persist and last
Trepidation and penalties have been cast

Imprints lasting in cement from sand
Intimacy so close like a glove on a hand
The dice are rolled, unknown how they will land

Secrets and deceit, leading to defeat
Two hearts that can never again meet

Betrayal deep into our core it seeps
Causing our inner spirit to die and weep
The lover's lover lives on, but not to keep

Pride can instill lasting shame and guilt
Blocking forgiveness and trust from being rebuilt

Only with God can once-promised unions be restored
Otherwise they will remain closed, shut, hollow doors
Then the former love dies and will be no more.

Get rid of all bitterness, rage and anger, brawling and slander, along with
every form of malice. Be kind and compassionate to one another, forgiving
each other, just as in Christ God forgave you.

EPHESIANS 4:31–32

ONLY WITH GOD

I BELIEVE THAT WE CAN HAVE GREAT joy while simultaneously holding great sorrow. We can be sad and happy at the same time; we do not have to be one or the other. Holding the tension of these opposite emotions heightens our human experience. Holding this tension of contrasting feelings is impossible for people but not for God. God can hold this tension for us, enabling us to feel joy while carrying deep sorrow. What is impossible for humans is not for God because with God all things are possible.

Unnecessary losses can make us weep
But sadness and joy we can both keep

Only with God

It is not "or," but "and"
Holding the opposites if we can

Just as the dark and sad
Give meaning to the light and glad

All the spectrums of feeling and emotion
Keep our humanness continuing in motion

Tears and smiles tie the perfect bow
Like fall and spring, we reap and sow

Opposites can be held together like one
Just as a day is a moon and a sun

Unnecessary losses can make us weep
But sadness and joy, we can both keep

Polar tensions lead to a balanced, vast life
Peace and contentment with no strife

Opposites we can hover between
Observing and noticing, not being drawn
into the scene

Diverging emotions live in broken hearts
The cracks allow them into the deepest parts

But it is only God who helps us contain
The tension of opposites and maintain

Suffering and joy, love and loss
Held together at our hearts' cost

With integration of the many into one
Diverse, complex capacity can come

Holding the opposites enhances and enriches
our lives even more
This is how our humanness can allow us
to soar

It is not about the one-dimensional "or,"
but the multidimensional "and"
Only with God, we will find we can.

Jesus looked at them and said, "With man this is impossible, but
with God all things are possible."

MATTHEW 19:26

TRUST GOD INTO THE ABYSS

AS A THERAPIST AND SPIRITUAL DIRECTOR, I often see psychological problems such as anxiety and depression originate from a distrust in God. When we do not trust God with our future, fear and worry begin to grow. Regrets from our past can also stem from a distrust in God's ability to forgive and give us a clean slate.

When we truly trust God, we can be fully present in our lives. We free ourselves from bondage, knowing true freedom in Christ.

I wrote this poem to express how trusting God releases us from our own self-imposed, personal world of suffering. It has been said if we take the leap, He will either catch us or teach us to fly.

Trusting God is leaping
into the abyss
Only to find and receive
His loving kiss

Trust God into the Abyss

Trusting God is leaping into the abyss
Only to find and receive His loving kiss

Fear and hurry fade away to no worry
Time stands still with no need to scurry

The tightness of anxiety dissolves
My trepidation quiets to resolve

The sadness has no place
As I focus only on my sweet Lord's face

Depression of the looming oppressive past
Falls away, removing my false, insecure mask

Confidence in a new day and a new way
Replace the lies of what my mind used to say

Joy and hope shine through
As I can and finally see God's truth

The dark clouds of night's disbelief
Give way, removing my sullen, morose grief

Solace is now to be found
Only God's word makes me sound

I reach into the blind night
Finding His hand to give me sight

Love and mercy in my heart prevail
I see myself no longer afraid and frail

God is there as always to lead me through
Though before I never trusted and knew

He is my shelter and my rock
I do not fear those crowds that mock

My salvation is safely resting in Him
I no longer place my security in them

The world can now never take my
*   given grace*
For my hope and faith are in my
*   Jesus's case*

So now I savor and move through life
Never fearing or frightened of any strife

Trusting in God is leaping into the abyss
Only to find and receive His loving kiss
This, my friend, you do not want to miss

Trust is one of God's most generous gifts
It is what raises me up and eternally lifts.

You will keep in perfect peace those whose minds are steadfast, because they trust in
you. Trust in the Lord forever, for the Lord, the Lord himself, is the Rock eternal.

Isaiah 26:3–4

THE PAST IS NEVER VERY FAR AWAY

WHEN WE RUN FROM FEELING OUR pain, it is only temporary relief; it is never a solution because the pain still remains within us. It is something that must be felt and processed. The pain of loss and grief must be experienced and felt. Otherwise it remains with us and will show up at some point in time as symptoms—psychological or physical. An event can trigger feelings from the past to surface because they were never allowed to be recognized and processed. We may think we have left the past behind, but suddenly it is with us again. It will remain until it can be discarded, which takes effort, work, and courage because it can be a painful process of expression. There is a time and a season to recognize, experience, and feel whatever we carry from the past. Then it can be let go and released back to the past and stay there. It then carries no power over us and we are set free.

Love is the bridge, the segue
This healing force opens the way

The Past Is Never Very Far Away

The past is never very far away
If not invited in, then it will stay

The pain and sorrow of the past
Can hover near and persistently last

Love is the bridge, the segue
This healing force opens the way

Pain leads to healing, goes hand in hand
Then stable, on our feet, is where we can land

To live and breathe down under the deep
Is the place where blessings are found to keep

So don't run away from your fear
Feel the grief and sorrow, draw them near

Slowly move through the suffering and the pain
Don't avoid it, then you will find the gain

Even the dark can have its gifts
Silver linings can be revealed when it lifts

The denied pain and sorrow living beneath
  your skin
Only torments and stifles your growth within

When unresolved and not recognized
It keeps you living and pretending a lie

The past will always show up uninvited
Taking you off guard if you're not farsighted

Unpack your baggage, leave it behind
This is the way to peace, you will find

The past is never very far away
Undivulged pain allows it to stay

There is a time for sorrow with its own season
In your life it has a purpose and reason

So put the past back in the past
Breathe through the pain, knowing it will
  not last.

Come to me, all you who are weary and burdened, and I will give you rest.

MATTHEW 11:28

ODE TO HEROIN

I AM THE PARENT OF A HEROIN addict.

I am writing as a parent that suffers from having a daughter who is a heroin addict.

I am not going to share her story because that is her journey. But her story has overflowed into my story and has traumatized me forever. I am a strong person, but heroin has broken me. I pray that none of you ever know the ravages and heartbreak of having a loved one who suffers from heroin addiction, because it is like confronting Satan—who wants to maim, kill, and destroy, and will probably win—face-to-face.

I am a physician, so one would think I have seen everything—and I have, but I cannot express the heartbreak and trauma that one experiences when you find your daughter clinically dead. I feel God prepared me to be a physician so at that specific moment in time I was able to save my precious girl.

I almost lost my beautiful daughter, but then a few years later I lost my oldest son from shallow water blackout, which has been another journey with trying to save lives through www.shallowwaterblackoutprevention.org.

Then my daughter, who had been doing so well and really excelling, had a huge emotional and physical setback. ER doctors readily handing out pain pills culminated in a relapse that ended with me finding her blue and unconscious from an overdose, her respiratory system compromised. By sheer divine intervention, I found her again. I should not have been at our house. I wasn't supposed to be, but I had a few minutes and ran by to check on my dogs. The trauma of finding my daughter a second time clinically dead has moved me to bravely speak out about the ravages of heroin addiction—not only on the victims but also on the families.

Heroin crosses all socioeconomic groups and has become an epidemic in the United States. I am a victim who lives in fear each day of finding her beautiful, perfect daughter dead or hearing she has died. I can no longer stay silent because her addiction has permanently traumatized me; so, this is part of my narrative, not just hers, and it has become my right and privilege to share and tell. I wish this was not so, but this is how I live my life.

My daughter, by God's grace, is now in recovery—a reality for which I am thankful every day. The apprehension of relapse is something I live with, but, as she does, I face each day one day at a time.

I send love and blessings to all the families of addicts who suffer daily with the trepidation of losing their loved one. It is our time to speak out to help stop addiction—especially heroin—that is killing so many amazing, gifted people and ravaging their families by depleting them mentally, emotionally, physically, and financially. Please have the courage to share your story because our voices together can change the world. When we can remove the shame, we can lessen our pain. God bless all of us.

You come to maim,
blame, shame, and destroy.
You rob of life, love,
trust, and joy.

Ode to Heroin

You come to maim, blame, shame, and destroy
You rob of life, love, trust, and joy

Your goal is Satan's work
And in the shadows, there he lurks

You play the sweet enticing sirens' song
Only too late to know it was all wrong

A moment's pain is gone
To only find it continues to go on and on

Your casualties are held captive by the links
*   of love and lure*
But sadly they discover there is no cure

They say heroin, the lover, is always there
Instantly ready to give and care

Lies, lies, and more lies are all you speak
Turning your victims into the weak

So goes the same old story every time
There is no reason nor rhyme

Death is there to shed his black cloak
As he watches young lives go up in his smoke

"Sinister" is too kind of word
Your evil voice should never be heard

You came to claim my child as your own
Never caring once for the loving family of
*   her home*
So though you have come and tread too near
I am not being pulled and lulled into your fear

My Lord is strong
And does no wrong

He will prevail
In the triumph of His nails

As long as there is life and breath
There is a battle to be fought and wept

You may think you win by stealing flesh
But Jesus does not leave his faithful to rest

Heaven's gates say it's not too late
God's paradise will certainly be her fate

The victory is already won
And you, Satan, remain forever under the Son

We will never give up, even if we must begin
Over and over, time again and again

In the final end
Heroin, you, and the devil will never, ever win.

The thief comes only to steal and kill and destroy; I have come that
they may have life, and have it to the full.

JOHN 10:10

NDUTU

I HAVE BEEN TO AFRICA, AND I find it captivating. The place is magical, beautiful, and alluring, but it also has a "heart of darkness." It is a land of life living with death. Life and death intertwined together, inseparable.

Ndutu is an area in the northern part of the Ngorongoro Conservation Area juxtaposed with the Serengeti in Tanzania. It conveys many feelings that Africa holds one needs to portray something to those who have the privilege to experience it. It fills me with complex and contradictory emotions. At the same time, the pure beauty of this natural world is mesmerizing and enticing. What I see is God's creation at its fullest, in its intricate simplicity and plan.

Life and Death are contiguous, juxtaposed
The circle of life is witnessed, proposed

✝

And God said, "This is the sign of the covenant I am making between me and you and every living creature with you, a covenant for all generations to come: I have set my rainbow in the clouds, and it will be the sign of the covenant between me and the earth. Whenever I bring clouds over the earth and the rainbow appears in the clouds, I will remember my covenant between me and you and all living creatures of every kind. Never again will the waters become a flood to destroy all life. Whenever the rainbow appears in the clouds, I will see it and remember the everlasting covenant between God and all living creatures of every kind on the earth."

GENESIS 9:12–16

Ndutu

There is a land like Xanadu
It is a place called Ndutu

It's where you can go back in time
Remembering what once was, a life now
   difficult to find

Nature here, you become a part
Viewing in close proximity, not from afar

You see into a mammoth, intricate,
   complex plan
One of order, balance, necessity, survival close
   at hand

A tranquil land of quiet beauty and serene peace
With roaming grasslands and plains that
   never cease

An end in sight your eye never meets
Touches within you a yearning, a drive to seek

A vast green sea seems to stretch to eternity
Farther and farther than the eye can see

Yellow ripples of swaying seed heads
This is the place where the striped zebra are led

The call of the rung-necked dove is the sound
   of the African song
The rufous-naped lark's sweet melody kindles
   your soul to long

A spectrum of colors, wildflowers to feast
A strange dichotomy seen compared to the
   fierce, untamed beasts

Life and death are contiguous, juxtaposed
The circle of life is witnessed, proposed

Deep emotions within you rattle and stir

This place romances, beckons, infatuates,
   and allures

But the hurt and suffering, the intense pain
Counterbalances the beauty to where there is
   no gain

The creatures are born with innately furled
   instinct
This drive is live, not die to become extinct

A strange sadness and morose melancholy
   it can evoke
The necessary sacrificial deaths, a conflicted
   grief it provokes

Life so short they never grow old
Legions and tales of the exceptions are the
   stories passed down and retold

Harmony and pugnacity are always on
   a delicate weighted scale
One moment there is triumph, then the
   next it can fail

God's paintings stretch broadly across
   the open skies
Time and space they try to defy

Crimson sunsets, pink sunrises, prism rainbows,
   and puffy white clouds passing by
Have you pondering the reasons why

Here nature is fully bared on display
A glimpse of Eden unspoiled, showing
   God's power and ways

The beauty is profound when experienced
   firsthand
The feelings are awe and wonder when
   witnessing God's plan.

THE QUESTION OF HELL

HELL CAN BE DESCRIBED AS THE ultimate, final confirmation of humanity's free will. God will never force us to be with Him; He will always allow us freedom to choose, just as we are always free to choose sin or not. As sin is separation from God, Hell is separation from God for eternity. It is everything that God is not. It is everything that Heaven is not. Heaven is without tears, pain, and suffering; so, Hell is the opposite with tears, pain, and suffering. Hell is being in darkness, not light; alone, not in community; without forgiveness, because God gives forgiveness; without love, as God is love; without joy and hope, as God's presence and promise give. Hell is then living with relentless regret that leads to sadness, hopelessness, and depression. Whatever God is, Hell is not. Whatever Heaven is, Hell is not. And there is no way out, not even by death, because this is eternity.

*Hell can be described
as the ultimate,
final confirmation of
humanity's free will.*

✝

God is light; in him there is no darkness at all.

1 John 1 :5

MORE ON THE QUESTION OF HELL

ON OUR DEATHBED WITH OUR LAST breath, we can decide if we do or do not want to be with God for eternity. But we can't fool God; He knows our true hearts. Many people delay dealing with God, thinking they have plenty of time; but sudden, unexpected death can rob them of that opportunity. If we ignore God in our daily lives, we are making a conscious choice not to be with Him. By thinking He does not exist or is not important, we choose an eternity separate from Him. That, my friend, is Hell. I personally don't ever want to experience my temporal or eternal life without God, because Hell can be in our afterlife or Hell can be here on earth. It's our choice to decide because we exercise our free will to choose our destiny, now and forever. May God grant us all willing spirits.

It's our choice to decide because we exercise our free will to choose our destiny, now and forever.

✝

Create in me a pure heart, O God, and renew a steadfast spirit within me. Do not cast me from your presence or take your Holy Spirit from me. Restore to me the joy of your salvation and grant me a willing spirit, to sustain me.

PSALM 51:10–12

AND GOD CRIED

I VISITED THE KIGALI GENOCIDE MEMORIAL IN Rwanda
and the Resistance Museum in Amsterdam. The stories of six million Jews and
one million Tutsis being exterminated because of their ethnicity drove me to
tears. Genocide is still occurring in many countries, and it must stop. This poem is a
reminder of what happens to humanity when genocide is allowed to persist. God cries
with us and for us.

I wrote this entire poem after visiting the museum in Rwanda while sitting in
its garden.

We all lose when we do not see
We are held accountable as our
minds remain free

And God Cried

People killing their neighbors and brothers
Maiming, slaughtering just because they are the others
Deep inside of us something then dies
From the echoes lingering of the screams and cries
With the devil they have shook his hands
By blindly obeying someone else's rhetoric and commands
There is a time to stand and defy
Denying, not believing the heinous lies

Discrimination and segregation are unfair
We must rise up, fight, and care
We are our brother's keepers, so we say
To live in peace is the only way
Otherwise, it can happen over and over again
If we don't listen but instead pretend
We must remember and never forget
If not, genocide we will live again to regret

Families destroyed and lives left broken
Winning the battle was the only token
Scars left outside and within
This is what remains, we must contend
Hatred will always breed hate
Then lost souls will be the case
At what sacrifice is the cost?
What within them and us has been lost?

Children can suffer for their father's sins

Then everyone loses, nobody wins
So many consequences and lessons to be learned
Trust and faith in others must be earned
Only with open forgiveness can lives find repair
Healing deep holes in hearts, unmended tears
Acceptance, kindness, love, and hope
Given to one another is the only solution to cope

Mistakes made can make it too late
Then cast to the wind our dismal fate
They become we and we become them
Then all our lives become dark, desolate, and grim
Malice and contempt, souls can mold
As hearts and spirits grow forever cold
We all lose when we do not see
We are held accountable as our minds remain free

His creation pitting man against man
Something He does not want or understand
This was never God's intention
The reason Jesus came and His Great Commission
So we must never surrender our voice
It remains always our pivotal choice
We may give up our lives in the end
But true to our conscience is the message we send

Heaven will spill over with tears
Until mankind learns over the years

Forgiving allows for reconciliation and healing
The promise of hope assuages the hurt and
  painful feelings
It is about loving each other, one and all
Otherwise we remain lost from the Fall
Sometimes we can't understand the reasons why

But we know God still weeps with us and sighs
And God cried and cries
Over the tragedy of human genocide.

✝

He answered, "'Love the Lord your God with all your heart and with all your soul and
with all your strength and with all your mind'; and, 'Love your neighbor as yourself.'"

LUKE 10:27

THIS SIDE OF HEAVEN

RECENTLY, MY LIFE JOURNEY HAS BEEN full of painful stories. Loves lost and unexplained tragedies have triggered thoughts and remembrances of my own deep heartbreak and loss. I also bear witness that even though love may pale with the loss of your beloved, the love you shared will always remain when that person is carried in your heart. I have learned to rest in the mystery, accepting that there are things in this life I will never understand. If you have experienced the untimely death of a loved one and the pain of love abruptly taken away, then you know there are some things we will never understand this side of Heaven.

You will make it through,
no need to escape

Just one day at a time, no
need to quicken the pace

This Side of Heaven

There are some things this side of Heaven we
   will never understand
Things so painful to endure you think you
   can't withstand

No reason, no logic can explain the Why
Every morning you wake up, praying it's been a lie

Numbness and denial are the zombie friends
You keep praying every moment the suffering will end

Tears flow down like an endless brook
Memories encircle with each remembered look

To move even a muscle is an effort lost
The persistent images remain at a cost

Too painful to remember but too cherished to forget
You wish time could be lost, could be reset

You think it could, would be easier to die
Than to continue breathing with each desperate sigh

The intimacy and connection you so deeply miss
Longs for one more gentle touch and tender kiss

Their lingering presence is like a shroud
Dense shadows cover you, harboring a black cloud

Reflected images in the mirrored glass
Give you glimpses of what was lost, gone in the past

You thought the storybook story would always last
But those frozen moments have melted, vanished too fast

The hourglass sand has kept on dripping
While your bleeding heart is torn, still ripping

The Piper continues to play His long song
But you know now the present is all wrong

You keep thinking of what you have been denied
Within your innermost being you want to defy

The wistful, solemn looks make you want to hide
You know this journey will be a long, rocky ride

Strength, courage, honor, the right thing to do
But you have lost your heart, you know you lose

If only the clock could turn back for a different choice
Then your heart's desire could have a different voice

So you must choose to go on living
Its duty, sacrifice, you must be willing

For all those you love are counting on you
Where to find the strength, if only you knew

The sting and bite of the reality now heard
The only place to turn, God's written word

In His healing presence you find your solace
   and life source
He encourages you and guides you back on
   the straight narrow course

So it is God you trust and gives you the
   patience to wait
The answer will come; it won't be too late

You will make it through, no need to escape
Just one day at a time, no need to quicken the pace

Sitting in this mystery with a mask of unknowing
All the while your faith and belief are
   continually growing

God promises He can redeem
No matter the sorrow or how it may seem

So in this sadness you may find your strength
Keep your courage in the pain, no matter the length

But you wish this heartbreak and loss would
  go away
You don't know or think there is a way

Secrets are choices that count and hurt
Then too late to change, no compromise, you assert

Entwined and furled together are love and loss
No separation, it is worth the cost

There are some things this side of Heaven we
  will never understand
But until, God will hold you up, never letting
  go of your hand

One day in the promised future, you will meet
  again in a different time, place, and land
You will look face-to-face and then know, because
  in Heaven you will stand.

For now we see only a reflection as in a mirror; then we shall see face to face. Now I
know in part; then I shall know fully, even as I am fully known.

1 CORINTHIANS 13:12

WALK ON

WHEN LIFE IS HARD, AND YOU face challenges, with God's help you can walk on. The sun will rise and there will be another day. Things will get easier if you can walk on.

*God's promise is to give you
a future and hope
He is constant and there to
help you cope*

Walk On

When times are tough, so hard to bear
You feel as if there is no one to care
Walk on

Those cloudy, dark days that seem to entrap
 and overwhelm
You feel as if God is no longer guiding your helm
Walk on

When hope seems to fade into the night
You don't think things will ever be right
Walk on

You are not sure you know what to do
You are searching everywhere, but you haven't
 a clue
Walk on

When you find yourself falling into a deep,
 bottomless hole
You have strayed and faltered no longer in
 the fold
Walk on

You feel discouraged, having lost your way
Everything has fallen apart to your dismay
Walk on

When your energy is depleted, diminishing
 your own life force
You have drifted aimlessly, wandering off course
Walk on

Remember God is always close and there
He will always take your burdens up to share
Walk on

He will keep you near and close in His sight
He is there for you to shed His light
Walk on

Don't worry and fret about the tomorrows
Release to Him all your burdens and sorrows
Walk on

Keep holding your head high and always try
Remember the sun keeps on shining, even with
 a gray sky
Walk on

God's promise is to give you a future and hope
He is constant and there to help you cope
Walk on

Just keep putting one foot in front of the other
The final finish line is closer not further
Walk on

Even if you think you can't, know you can
Keep your belief trusting in God to hold your hand
And
Walk on.

I can do all things through him who gives me strength.

PHILIPPIANS 4:13

BEHIND THE SMILE

T HOUGH THIS POEM AND THE STORY I'm about to tell describe my own experience, I know that the feeling of believing we're less than others is a universal experience for so many and relative to our individual life circumstances. I look back now, realizing I was very blessed in what I was given, including opportunities and experiences others have never had. But this poem is for you, if you have ever felt less than anyone else.

This poem and its title, "Behind the Smile," is very personal to me. When I was a young girl in eighth grade, I was a new student. I was very self-conscious because I didn't have the wealth of my friends at this academically excellent private school. My idea was to always smile and appear happy to have friends.

During the first week in science class, my teacher asked each student to write on an index card their thoughts and impressions of the classmate whose name appeared on the card; the class was then to guess who the card was about. My teacher read a card about a girl who always had a smile on her face, but the writer of the card commented that they wondered what was really behind that smile and what it may have been covering up. The girl described on the card was me. It embarrassed and hurt me that others could see behind my smile. I had always worked so hard to keep a happy face, in spite of the fact that I carried a lot of pain: I was from a divorced home; my dad was an alcoholic; my mother worked hard to help pay my tuition, and she didn't have a lot of money to buy me the same kinds of clothes or items other girls around me had; my home was modest; and so on. There were things to hide behind my smile, but I still put it on every day, no matter the circumstance. I thought that if I tried hard enough, my smile would become reality.

It took many years of tough life experiences, some therapy, and much growth in my faith for me to have the courage to remove that mask. I now am not ashamed of who I am and where I came from, as this journey has made me the person I am. God doesn't waste a single tear or any of our pain and hurt. He uses them to mold us into something beautiful. So, I stand tall and walk in transparency today, being the only person I could ever be, and that's the me God created me to be. I still smile a lot, but it is no longer the fake mask I used to wear.

As fog stained mirrors, the truth it eludes
That painted fake grimace will cover the mood

Behind the Smile

What lurks in the mind's corners, behind the smile?
Pain, hurt, shame, guilt, thoughts that self-defile
One may not see, but they live there all the while

You tell yourself put on your best face,
And you must make it in haste
For time is fleeting, don't let it waste

You must keep that smile, no allowed tears
Day after day living with uncertain mocking and fears
A toll it takes on the soul over the many years

As fog stained mirrors, the truth it eludes
That painted fake grimace will cover the mood
If the veracity were known, you it would exclude

Somber secret sadness creeps behind the pretend mask
Keeping it hidden is a relentless burdensome task
God can heal this if you can and will just ask

Clocks keep ticking on toward the future so very fast
But with honesty and acceptance, a new destiny can be cast
When surrendered to the truth as no smile can forever really last.

✝

For you created my inmost being; you knit me together in my mother's
womb. I praise you because I am fearfully and wonderfully made; your works
are wonderful, I know that full well.

PSALM 139:13–14

TEARS BENEATH

I HAVE OFTEN WRITTEN ABOUT MY TWENTY–FIVE–YEAR-OLD son who died in April of 2011, because he remains an impactful subject of my writings. The years have assuaged the pain, but underneath it still remains. I carry tears just beneath the surface. At the same time, I go on through life continuing to enjoy each day as a gift from God.

Deep loss never really leaves us. It becomes integrated into our very being and part of who we are. There can be a blessing attached; in that, through our experience we can become a more sensitive and compassionate person. The suffering ignites growth within us. I know for myself when I look back at the person I was, I feel thankful for the person I am today despite the pain of loss. That is not to say I am glad my son died—I wish him back every day, but I can thank God for the blessing of the person I have become.

Fleeting years have long passed, gone by
Every day I still question the reasons why

Tears Beneath

My tears remain under the surface just beneath
Their presence has meaning, meant to teach
I have since gotten used to living this way
They have their own mind and will, I don't have a say

On the outside you may see smiles that I send
I still feel joy and happiness, it's not pretend
But underneath, the sorrow still lurks and lives
Depth of feeling, empathy, and compassion to me it gives

Oddly this grief is my old friend I know so well
Lives and breathes a secret blessing I want to share and tell

You say wouldn't I give up wearing this dark badge of loss?
As I have endured this pain and suffering at such great cost

Fleeting years have long passed, gone by
Every day I still question the reasons why
But who I am today I would not be
I now have the special gifts to acutely hear and see

So in God's loving mercy and grace
I can thrive, though I no longer see my beloved's face
I place all my trust and faith in serving Him
Through God each day, I am able to start and begin again.

He has sent me to bind up the brokenhearted, to proclaim freedom for the captives and release from darkness for the prisoners, to proclaim the year of the Lord's favor and the day of vengeance of our God, to comfort all who mourn and provide for those who grieve in Zion—to bestow on them a crown of beauty instead of ashes, the oil of joy instead of mourning, and a garment of praise instead of a spirit of despair. They will be called oaks of righteousness, a planting of the Lord for the display of his splendor.

ISAIAH 61:1–3

A SEASON FOR ALL THINGS

I N LIFE THERE ARE TIMES OF sadness and sorrow along with joy and happiness. There is a season for all things in life. This is part of our human journey. All emotions and feelings are part of our human experience as God created us to have a spectrum. This is what it means to be human. They are neither good nor bad; feelings are products of our emotions.

Emotions are primary and instinctual, while feelings are subjective mental associations and reactions. Our feelings are ours and do not need justification but validation. To accept all our emotions without judgment is to embrace our humanness. If we sit with our emotions, they will change; they will not remain constant. So, there is a time for sadness and a time for joy. For every time there is a season.

Just as the seasons never stay the same, life always changes. The different seasons bring life and growth and then degeneration and death. Death can give way to rebirth with newness and regeneration. So, as we accept the time for all things, we must finally in our hearts surrender to accepting God's infinite plan and its goodness.

Birth and death, beginnings and ends
What matters in life are the messages we send

A Season for All Things

People may come into our lives for a season
And when we reflect there was a purpose
   and reason
All those leave an indelible imprint on who
   we become
But we are still more than just all of the sums

There will be sadness, suffering, and loss
Love is always worth this cost
A season for growth and change
Then things will never be the same

A time to let go of the past
Realizing nothing but love will ever last
We will grow old as the circle of life continues
Nothing is for free, we all pay our dues

Birth and death, beginnings and ends
What matters in life are the messages we send
Heroes and heroines come and go
All are still mortal with all life's woes

We are all just tiny grains of sand
Not knowing when or where we may land
So live each moment with joy and appreciation
As our entire life is this final culmination

When we look at all the beauty and really see
Then we can know God's goodness is what's
   meant to be
God has a time and season for all His plans
Finally we must trust that we are safe in
   His loving hands.

✝

He has made everything beautiful in its time. He has also set eternity in the human heart; yet no one can fathom what God has done from beginning to end. I know that there is nothing better for people than to be happy and to do good while they live. . . . I know that everything God does will endure forever; nothing can be added to it and nothing taken from it. God does it so that people will fear him. Whatever is has already been, and what will be has been before; and God will call the past to account.

ECCLESIASTES 3:11–12, 14–15

PART FOUR

———

Hope

NEW BEGINNINGS

JANUARY IS THE FIRST MONTH OF the new year. It is a time for reflection and change, a time to alter things that we need to let go of, those parts that hold us back. But, as we look closer into the microcosm, it is not just January but each day that offers a new beginning to find, to live, and to begin a new way . . . always, every day.

*Each day is a new
beginning
With possibilities
never-ending*

New Beginnings

Each day is a new beginning
With possibilities never-ending

Hope awaits on the horizon
Life may brighten and enlighten

A new chance for a new way
Each and every new day

Just as the seed sprouts forth to grow
Rebirth can be what we know

We must keep the faith
Knowing it is never too late

The future may be found safe
We can survive it unscathed

We have to let go of the past
As change is what will always last

There is nothing left to fear
Though death always hovers near

We all live teetering on the rope
So let God be the One to help us cope

God's hope is the promised game
Only His forgiveness can remove our shame

So let all apprehension be put to rest
Life is not a test or about being the best

Take each day, one day at a time
Letting go of every single past crime

Releasing those past sins
Gives us a new way to begin

Most all our worries dwell in our mind
So a silver lining is ours to find

If we can start over one more time
Everything will work out just fine

All our living days hold a new sunrise
Where hope rests before our eyes

Live each day as it might be our last
Time is fleeting by so very fast

Be present fully to feel, hear, and see
Mindful living will be the key

Remain in the moment of life
Relinquishing all the world's turmoil and strife

Then choose to trust God always first
He will be there to quench our thirst

The three: faith, hope, and love
The fourth: belief in our Father above

A new year, a new day, with new beginnings
Old ways are gone with their endings

It's always time to begin anew
Each new year or day, a chance to renew

And then next year or tomorrow once more begin
Living life, beginning over and over again.

Therefore do not worry about tomorrow, for tomorrow will worry about itself.

MATTHEW 6:34

BE STILL

ALTHOUGH HE IS ALWAYS WITH ME, I often need just to *be* to feel His presence in the stillness and quiet. Being is an intentional act that draws us closer and nearer to God. It is a movement toward God. Being is releasing oneself to be fully present to the moment, which is where we meet God. It is being present in the present. With Him there is always hope.

*Being is an intentional act that
draws us closer and nearer to God.*

Be still and know that I am God.

Psalm 46:10

A MOMENT IN TIME

WE LIVE LIFE TO THE FULLEST when we are present in and to the moment. It is actually the only reality we really have. It is also when God meets us in a moment in time, the vertical intersecting the horizontal. God brings eternity into the moment as He meets us. So, cherish it and don't miss it—don't miss God. That is where He lives and waits.

Time is fleeting sand
in the hourglass
Impossible to not
make it pass

215

A Moment in Time

All that really exists is the moment
There is no need for the past to ever torment

The past is the past
It will not and cannot last

Being present to the present
Ceases all reason for morose lament

Time idles and freezes to the second
The mind's crafty teasers lure and beckon

Anxiety is the stealthy robber's secret
That knows no bounds or egress

It is the "is" of the present tense
Living with each breath abets sense

Time is fleeting sand in the hourglass
Impossible to not make it pass

The moment can never be thrown away
    or cast
Impervious, futile catching time as it
    speeds so fast

The past only remains a prequel
With each moment there is no sequel

The moment vanishes regret
There is no furtive agenda to fret

The plaudits are held in cursory reality
There is no rehearsal or duality

The future and past become banal and fraught
The present moment is the lesson to be taught

It is only the now to be here
Because the specter death is always lurking near

It is where God always meets us in the end
The great Vertical is who into time descends

So come live in the moment and be with me
This is the only place where we live, breathe,
    and see

A moment in time holds the past, present, and
    future in one
It is what determines the person we become

✝

Show me, Lord, my life's end and the number of my days; let me know how fleeting
my life is. You have made my days a mere handbreadth; the span of my years is as
nothing before you. Everyone is but a breath, even those who seem secure.

PSALM 39:4–5

216

GRATITUDE

WITH PRAISE AND THANKSGIVING TO GOD. We will receive hope and blessings.

Thankful for a sowed harvest now to reap
Joyful sounds from our spirits leap

Gratitude

Willing hearts that can speak
Within our souls, humility running deep
Praising God with prayers as we seek
Giving thanks even while we weep
Thankful for a sowed harvest now to reap
Joyful sounds from our spirits leap
Even when we hurt with wounds that seep
Moving toward God even though we creep

In quiet and stillness His voice we will hear
He will wipe away every single tear
We will never be afraid or have fear
No matter the outcome with God it cannot scare

To His heart we are held close and dear
He paid the price, He made it clear
The Kingdom is now, it is right here
It is gratitude to God that draws us near

Trusting God with our souls to keep
Not fearing the future in our sleep
Lessons we learn then must teach
Thankful hearts overflow to help the weak
Pride released to become humble and meek
Gratitude allows redemption to be reached
Glimmers and glimpses of Heaven can then leak
Grateful to God for the blessings given to each.

Praise the Lord, my soul; all my inmost being, praise his holy name. Praise the Lord, my soul, and forget not all his benefits—who forgives all your sins and heals all your diseases, who redeems your life from the pit and crowns you with love and compassion, who satisfies your desires with good things so that your youth is renewed like the eagle's.

PSALM 103:1–5

PEACE

I WROTE THIS POEM TO WISH PEACE on the world, knowing that peace begins first with each one of us, in our own hearts. May the peace of God that surpasses all understanding remain with us always, and may it spread throughout the world, bringing peace to all. Let your light shine bright for all to see.

God waits patiently to love and forgive
Harmony and joy are the gifts His peace gives

Peace

The feeling of calm when all heads are spinning
Never based on conquering or winning
But on a heart that stays open and willing

Through shining eyes are seen God's light
Giving the ability to sleep all through the night
Knowing there is never a reason to hate or fight

Despite all anxiety, worry, and fears
It lasts even as we grow old over the years
Still forgiving and loving through shed tears

Something no human may ever understand
Forbearance to bear pain and withstand

Knowing Heaven is the future promised land

This peace of God centers, making us stable
With confidence we know that we are able
With Him and through Him, we are capable

The peace and strength are all His
He remains unchanged and always is
He wants our hearts, but does not insist

God waits patiently to love and forgive
Harmony and joy are the gifts His peace gives
It is because within our hearts the Savior lives!

And the peace of God, which transcends all understanding,
will guard your hearts and your minds in Christ Jesus.

PHILIPPIANS 4:7

WHAT IF?

I WROTE "WHAT IF?" AS A REMINDER to focus on the present and future possibilities and opportunities that God has for us when we trust and rely on Him. So often during my counseling sessions, I see clients who get stuck in the past with regret and what could have been—the what-ifs. The past cannot be changed, so it must be processed, accepted, and learned from, because mistakes are the best teachers in life. Being able to let go of the past and move forward is essential for one to receive the gifts of the present and the gifts of the future that God has in store for us. "To dream forward with hope, vision, and strategy / Abiding in God's eternal plan holds the key." Remember all things are possible with God.

Not "what if," but "what
is" and "what can be"
To look, know, and see all
the possibilities

What If?

Those thoughts and fantasies that live in the cobwebs
  of our minds
They echo in the darkness thoughts of every kind
The foggy shadows cast may stay, not lift
They haunt and speak, "What if?"

The words spoken are regret then sadness and sorrow
They rob the joy, zest, and zeal of tomorrow
This catatonia can paralyze, sucking breath and life
In our hearts the dualism causes tension and strife

The mind's broken record plays over and over again
Can these severed bridges of regret ever find mend?
Each moment, each decision, each mistake
Is it too late, will it seal our fate?

"What if" are things that never were
The past is past, it can't recur
"What is" is present now
To consciously, mindfully, intentionally live somehow

The past cannot, will not be changed

No matter the consequences it remains the same
It is with patience and acceptance, the need to wait
Trusting in God and His promise to never forsake

Not looking backward, but facing and turning forward
With belief and faith a new door will be opened by
  the Lord
The old door is closed, shut, locked, not to be opened
This is the case, the truth, not a mere notion

Can we touch our dreams without rejection and recoil
  from reality?
When we have willing ears to listen and eyes to see
There is God's scheme where things don't need to
  turn around
Where meaning and significance can still be found

Not "what if," but "what is" and "what can be"
To look, know, and see all the possibilities
To dream forward with hope, vision, and strategy
Abiding in God's eternal plan holds the key.

Whoever has ears, let them hear what the Spirit says to the churches. To the one who is
victorious, I will give the right to eat from the tree of life, which is in the paradise of God.

REVELATION 2:7

RISE UP

GOD CREATED US WITH AN INVINCIBLE human spirit that can rise from the ashes to victory. We can be victors, not victims. We can be overcomers with our God-given human will, strength, and determination. This hope God built into our DNA to cause us, no matter the circumstance, to be able to rise up.

Trust in God

takes away

our fear

His promise is not

to forsake, but to

stay near

What, then, shall we say in response to these things?
If God is for us, who can be against us?

ROMANS 8:31

Rise Up

The human spirit will never die
Like the phoenix from the fire it will rise

From the ashes a crown of beauty is received
The heavenly glory to come will satisfy all our needs

A hundred times the child may stumble and fall
But he will learn to run, leaving his crawl

This is something that can never be taken or sold
In us, it is courage and character it molds

It was built into us to always strive
This is what allows our humanity to survive and thrive

We forever aspire to the formidable heights
We never surrender the ineluctable fight

Wars, obstacles, and bondage cannot defeat
But they separate the strong from the weak

The key is held in the power of our minds
It is strength of will and determination to find

Wisdom and discernment keep us knowing
But, heart and soul are what will keep us going

Trust in God takes away our fear
His promise is not to forsake, but to stay near

It is in the Spirit we are not victims but victors
It is He who redeems, rebuilds, and restores

We can become worriers or warriors
We can plunge, crash, or soar

Let us rise up, be on fire and fly
There is no limit, not even the sky

If God is for us, no one can stand against us
So rise up, rise up, no choice, we must
Rise up, rise up, in God we trust.

WONDER

THE WORLD THAT SURROUNDS US IS full of wonder and wonderful things. There is also a wide range of feelings and emotions to experience. There are so many things to wonder about and consider.

Wondering is the act of desiring or having curiosity to know about something or the answer to a question. It is considering the possibilities and the options. It keeps us open, growing, and in excited anticipation. I am a wonderer. Do you ever wonder? Are you a wonderer, too?

I wonder if
People are really all the same
Just different covers, playing life's game?

Wonder

Do you ever wonder?
I wonder if
All the stars and galaxies are alone
Or are they someone or something's home?

Do you ever wonder?
I wonder if
Within all this intricate plan and design
Are there answers to explain and find?

Do you ever wonder?
I wonder if
Things we cannot see, but only feel
Are they what should be most valued
   and real?

Do you ever wonder?
I wonder if
Love can be timeless and spaceless
Lasting when your lover is distant,
   intangible, and faceless?

Do you ever wonder?
I wonder if
People are really all the same
Just different covers, playing life's game?

Do you ever wonder?
I wonder if

Living creatures feel human emotions
That sadness and pain produce for them
   doleful inner commotions?

Do you ever wonder?
I wonder if
There is uncompromising universal truth
Standing outside of time, not remote or aloof

Do you ever wonder?
I wonder if
Dreams, wishes, and prayers can really come true
And are there answers to mysteries, can we
   perceive the clues?

Do you ever wonder?
I wonder if
There is meaning and significance for each
   one of us
Knowing with confidence in God's plan we
   can trust?

Do you ever wonder?
I wonder if
When God knows our true hearts seeing
   the good
Will we be forgiven our sin, do we think
   He could?

Now faith is confidence in what we hope for and assurance about what we do not see.

HEBREWS 11:1

IMMORTALITY

IS DEATH REALLY THE END? I think not if we believe God's promises and His word. There is eternal life. Life will go on, and it will be even better than our best day on earth.

We are eternal spiritual beings moving through
A temporal perishable world waiting to be reborn
and made new

Immortality

Where does the period and new sentence begin?
It varies with each, but there is never really an end
Just a transition from that to this
But a somber immortality is what we risk

Energy goes on, never lost, but transformed
Means we are not dying from the moment born
Oh, how our simple minds cannot conceive
What does it really mean to live and to be?

Here life and living are such a brief sojourn
Death is temporary, no need to mourn
After the comma, a brief pause, then we see
There is no real period or end for you or me

Like a mere drop of water in the sea
Joined together we make one unity
Just as the lone solitary blade of grass
Conforms and grows into a single mass

Each person you have touched also changes your life
Together our interaction is what makes us blithe
Just as each unique puzzle piece fits together
  in union
This sharing of love becomes our communion

His eternal plan holds and reveals our fate
Like a giant jigsaw, it makes a picture, vast and great

He allows us to choose; it is never too late
God does all of this from love for our
  own sake

What lies beneath and within
Holds and hides our deepest sin
But love is able to conquer all
God will draw us into Him then enthrall

Molecules can rearrange
Appearances may then change
What once was will be no more
We become glorified bodies made to soar

When we hear the trumpet music floating
  in the air
It will confirm and acknowledge God has
  always been there
God created us for Him and immortality
His Son makes this possible for all a reality

Forever is what the eye just can't see
It is the place, land, dimension of eternity
We are eternal spiritual beings moving through
A temporal perishable world waiting to be
  reborn and made new.

However, as it is written: "What no eye has seen, what no ear has heard, and what no human mind has conceived"—the things God has prepared for those who love him—

1 CORINTHIANS 2:9

THE YEARNING

EVEN DURING OUR HAPPIEST MOMENTS, WE never feel totally complete. There is something missing, lacking, not totally satisfied. As we become still and quiet, we can feel with each heartbeat a yearning, a calling for home.

There is a longing and desire that always remains for something more than what is. It is to return to our Creator, to be once more pure, complete, and whole. This yearning is for our origin, our true home. So for now, we hold the tension of our yearning, waiting, as the best is yet to come. I wrote this poem with these thoughts in mind.

Finally to be completely accepted and known
Our hearts will be satisfied, never again to roam

The Yearning

There is something within us, a longing, a yearning
In our hearts is this smoldering flame always burning
There is no complete contentment or peace
Because we are not home, there remain feelings of loss
  and grief
We get remote brief glimmers every now and then
Otherwise, we continue to make believe and pretend
It is to be totally whole and complete
That we are unable to obtain and meet
This desire remains kindled not winced
This thirst cannot be satisfied or quenched

As we grow older, we grow closer to our real home
It is only there we will never feel sad or alone
Finally to be completely accepted and known
Our hearts will be satisfied, never again to roam
For now we only see glimpses partly
Because we still see through the glass darkly
The veil will one day be removed to clearly see
Our souls will then take flight, be set free
So until then our angels, solace they will send
Death gives no period, but a comma as there is no end
Amen.

Look to the Lord and his strength; seek his face always.

1 CHRONICLES 16:11

METAPHORS OF RESURRECTION

IN NATURE, METAPHORS OF RESURRECTION POINT to rebirth, transformation, and afterlife, ultimately pointing to the resurrection of Jesus Christ. One of the most miraculous is the transformation of the humble caterpillar into a beautiful butterfly. The little creature chooses to take its own life, encasing itself in a cocoon. The tiny body becomes a corpse and completely dissolves, becoming a chrysalis. This chrysalis becomes the butterfly, then the new creature must break out of its cocoon. During this process of breaking and stretching, the butterfly struggles to make its wings strong to fly. This process is a miracle. It is purposeful, as metamorphosis does not conserve energy. God has built this beautiful process into nature to teach us many things, but the most important is about the resurrection of Christ and eternal life.

There are Metaphors of Resurrection if we don't just look, but see
Viewing nature through God's lens is the key

Metaphors of Resurrection

There are metaphors of resurrection if we don't
   just look, but see
Viewing nature through God's lens is the key

Butterflies arising from an encased tomb
Breaking free to flutter from their dark room

A vanishing Houdini, a chrysalis makes
This lost death God does not forsake

Rebirth to a new life, now transformed
Cloaked in beauty all fanciful and adorned

Crawling creature now born to be free
Flying and soaring so high, just to be

No reason, no rhyme, this does not make sense
God has His purpose; He does not once wince

Little tadpole, a swimming aquatic, darting in a pool
Then legs you grow, now on the ground you rule

Terrestrial amphibian those whinges you emote
Once ago in silence, your voice was remote

You grow and change before our eyes
Surely God must have some reason why

Water bugs living down under with no air
Then it is translucent wings you don and wear

Dragonflies take to your aerial flight
Only to live and breathe for a brief fortnight

An ethereal creation such complexity, it insists
Resurrection metaphors do in nature exist

Dubious death and changed forms
Are actually creation's way and the norm

In metamorphosis God does teach
Saying there can be many images for each

The old form dies and is then lost
With rebirth there is always a cost

Life goes on living in a new state
It means eternal life will be our future fate

All these types and symbols point to Easter Day
When Jesus, our Savior, came to show us the way

Death He conquered from which He rose
To save our lives, His fate He chose

God has sent a message that is clear to read
But He leaves it for us to decide, to take heed

Be present to each moment surrounding us
Marking and noting each clue, we must

For man, God has made it so plain
All Heaven and Earth are His eternal reign

God has shown us; He wants to be fair
These metaphor gifts are because of His care

So when we see clearly and do not err
Then God's metaphors of resurrection can be
   found everywhere.

But the Advocate, the Holy Spirit, whom the Father will send in my name, will teach
you all things and will remind you of everything I have said to you.

JOHN 14:26

AFTERLIFE KISSES

RED CARDINALS ARE SPECIAL BIRDS REPRESENTING God's love and comfort. They also represent Christ's blood as they were named after the cardinals in the Roman Catholic Church who wear red as the symbol of Christ's blood. My son, Whitner, died on Palm Sunday 2011. I was sent a red cardinal a few days after his death when I boldly asked God for a sign that my son was with Him. The red bird lit next to me. Since that time my yard has seen an infestation of cardinals—that would be my son drawing all the attention! They always show up when I need comfort, affirmation, or love. Their call is very distinct, so even if I don't see them I know they are with me as I know my invisible God is always with me. So if my Whitner is with God, and God is always with me, then my son is always with me. Such a blessing and affirmation to know God often sends the red cardinal to give love and comfort to others, too. The red bird is a healing presence from God and our loved ones. I call these gifts of love "afterlife kisses."

My story about the red cardinal has received a lot of interest as others have shared visits of love from these beautiful red birds. I also have had many other love messages, from finding pennies and dimes to the presence of rainbows, butterflies, dragonflies, tree frogs, and doves; besides the male red cardinals, I also get females. I wrote a poem about these afterlife kisses.

Guardian angels sending their love
Precious gifts from Heaven above

Afterlife Kisses

Pennies, dimes, coins abound
So many that I have found

Guardian angels sending their love
Precious gifts from Heaven above

Raindrops to rainbows in skies I see
Signs of hope and promise given to me

Falling feathers drifting down
Tell me you are safe and sound

Yellow butterflies of resurrection
Rebirth is our hope and conception

Ethereal dragonflies bringing eternal light
Come to me as solace for my dark night

Tree frogs that have been transformed
Showing life does change, is not conformed

A pair of cooing mourning doves
Send me confirmation of everlasting love

The hidden red bird's melodious song
Reminds me you are not ever really gone

Love is this life source and prevailing force
That helps me to stay on this long, rocky course

Yes, it is you I will always forever miss
But the afterlife sends to me a tender God kiss

So although I no longer see your sweet face
I am blessed by God's merciful, loving grace.

The Lord your God is with you, the Mighty Warrior who saves. He will take great delight
in you; in his love he will no longer rebuke you, but will rejoice over you with singing.

ZEPHANIAH 3:17

WHEN THE VEIL BECOMES THIN

SINCE MY SON'S DEATH, I PERIODICALLY get signs of his love. They arrives as red cardinals, dragonflies, pennies, dimes, feathers, and so on. I call these signs "afterlife kisses." They appear when the veil between the spiritual realm and physical realm becomes so thin it is transparent, letting little pieces of Heaven slip through as gifts of love and comfort. I wait with anticipation for these special moments when the veil becomes thin.

When the veil becomes thin
The blessing from Heaven rains in

When the Veil Becomes Thin

At times the veil becomes very thin
Letting the eternal spiritual realm within

You make your ethereal presence known
Through this incantation my belief has grown

I am certain that life does go on
We will meet again; it won't be long

The transparent veil reveals Christ's face
It allows us to know and feel God's grace

Death is but a blink of the eye
It does not last; no need to cry

But I still miss your touch
And I still love you so much

The sadness looms from that day
The day of days you went away

I am afraid your image will fade
So I cling to memories, my mind's cascade

Thoughts of times gone by
Never again to meet my eye

They race beyond in a blurring scene
Soft specters dancing in my dream

I pause in silence for life to be
Seeking missed messages from you to me

Lost visions gone from sight
No actions or words make this right

So I hope and pray for a visit tonight
The conjured images, dreams take flight

You once were, but now no more
It's disbelief that shuts the door

I think you will return one day
So many words with so much to say

Your lingering presence, I need to stay
Please don't leave me, don't go away

Death is not so proud anymore
Its ugly head wants to even the score

Death will die and live no more
The angels in Heaven will wait then soar

So I remain guarded in the night
By my precious loved ones in the light

We all will witness the Great Fight
Our Lord on white steed victorious
*   with His might*

When the veil becomes thin
The blessing from Heaven rains in

Until then the incarnational tells the tale
Eternal everlasting love will prevail
So I wait quietly for the thin veil.

But whenever anyone turns to the Lord, the veil is taken away.

2 CORINTHIANS 3:16

THOUGHTS ON TRUTH

THE TRUTH IS ALWAYS THE TRUTH. It is just waiting to be discovered. The truth is the truth. It stands outside of time. It never changes. It remains the same through the centuries. It is only we who change as truth is revealed to us and discovered by us. It was and is and will be always there waiting to be found. God is forever the truth-holder.

The truth is always the truth.
It is just waiting to be discovered.

†

Jesus Christ is the same yesterday and today and forever.

HEBREWS 13:8

WE ARE EITHER MOVING TOWARD GOD OR AWAY FROM GOD

I N EACH MOMENT OF EVERY DAY, we are choosing to move toward God or away from Him. By not exerting intention, we will drift away from God. Just as when we are floating on top of the ocean, we will drift out to sea away from the shore. But, with exertion and intention, we can swim safely to shore.

Each day is an opportunity to move closer to God, growing in the intimacy of our relationship with Him; it is always a choice to be intentional, as God is always there waiting to be in communion, communing in union, with us. He waits at the door, knocking, asking for us to invite Him in.

Here I am! I stand at the door and knock. If anyone hears my voice and
opens the door, I will come in and eat with that person, and they with me.

REVELATION 3:20

BARREN PEAKS AND LUSH VALLEYS

ON THE BARREN PEAKS OF MOUNTAINS above the tree line, there is no growth, but in the lush, fertile valleys there is abundant growth. Like the gardener who prunes his bushes, removing branches to get new healthy growth and to help the plant thrive and flourish, God uses our hurt and pain to make us stronger, growing us. So those painful cuts and deep valleys of life are what produce strength, growth, resilience, and fortitude. They develop us into who God created us to be. He does not waste even a single one of our tears. So, it is the pain and deep valleys of life that grow us, making us stronger. God can bring good from the worst suffering for those who love Him, for those who are His.

God uses our hurt and pain to make
us stronger, growing us.

✝

For he has rescued us from the dominion of darkness and brought us
into the kingdom of the Son he loves.

COLOSSIANS 1:13

GOD TURNS DARKNESS
INTO LIGHT

IT IS IN THOSE "DARK NIGHTS of the soul" that we grow the most, as God draws us near to Him. In the darkness at night when we sleep our body grows, heals, and repairs itself. Just as a seed needs darkness to grow and germinate, we need darkness.

We may feel abandoned and alone in the dark, but if we only blindly reach our hand out into the darkness with trust we will find God standing next to us with His outstretched hand, waiting to transform the darkness into light.

These are times that God can actually be closest to us, loving us, using the darkness to help us grow into a mature spiritual being.

He can transform our darkness into light.

You, Lord, are my lamp; the Lord turns my darkness into light.

2 SAMUEL 22:29

He can transform our darkness into light.

I MEET YOU, GOD

THIS POEM, "I MEET YOU, GOD," is about knowing God and who He is. We can experience God in so many ways, but especially in nature, which is His beautiful creation. There, in nature's peace, stillness, and solitude we can hear His voice.

God always meets us in the present moment, which is timeless. He carries eternity into the moment. This moves us toward union with holy God. Are you listening for God's voice in your heart and life?

The wind whispers Your beloved name
Constant, unchanging, staying always the same

I Meet You, God

Alone in my quiet place I am still
It is then my heart to overflowing You fill
As the gentle breeze grazes my skin
My soul opens up to let You in

The wind whispers Your beloved name
Constant, unchanging, staying always the same
The sea's roar proclaims Your strength and might
Since I now know You, I am no longer without sight

I see You in colored rainbow skies
It is for You my soul whimpers and cries
I experience You in the beauty of all nature
Your presence I know; I feel no danger

You have been, are, and will be there for me
Guiding my path with Your light to see
Patiently waiting and listening for You
All my needs You already knew

I know You from the love You send
Because You live and dwell within
Cool spring waters like You quench my thirst
From now on I promise to place You first

Rebirth has given me a brand-new life
Now I live with no contention or strife
I meet You, God; I meet Your Son
In the eternal moment we become one.

I the Lord do not change. So you, the descendants of Jacob, are not destroyed.

MALACHI 3:6

LIVING IN THE KINGDOM

MY FORMER PROFESSOR, DALLAS WILLARD, AT the Renovaré Institute said that when he dies he will hardly know the difference between Heaven and earth, as the Kingdom of God is here now. I view it as living in two worlds simultaneously with awareness of each, straddling the eternal spiritual realm and the temporal physical realm. I envision when I die, it will be like lifting one foot up and placing it next to the other. I will then be fully standing in Heaven, God's everlasting kingdom.

So often people become "saved" and "born again," but they stay stagnant in their Christian faith. Many do not understand that Kingdom living is every second of every day, not once a week on Sundays. We should live every moment with intention, making an effort to live a Christ-centered life.

I wrote the poem "Living in the Kingdom" to describe what living in God's kingdom every day is like.

God's eternal realm
exists with us now
To us His love and
grace He endows

260

Living in the Kingdom

Living in the Kingdom is done with intention
It is lived moment to moment with decision
It begins now when we are present and still
Transcending and accepting God's will

It is where Heaven begins
It is where our old life ends
Feeling deeply with intensity
Accepting life's unexplained mystery

Kingdom dwellers share in communion
Moving to God toward union
Valuing and appreciating each and every second
Listening and hearing the Holy Spirit's beckon

Our senses become heightened and attuned
Never again to feel lost and marooned
Growing spirituality is the goal
Gone are our former ways and old roles

Death is no longer a fear
We know Christ walks with us and is near
Never alone will we be
God's presence we feel and see

We come to trust God and His plan
Knowing He is there to always guide us by the hand
Love spills from our hearts, overflowing to all
Our souls lift in song to God, enthralled

Kingdom living brings joy and peace
Depression, anxiety, worry will then cease
God's eternal realm exists with us now
To us His love and grace He endows

Being Christ-centered is the Life and the
   Kingdom way
Holy Scripture's truth is the final say
Praise and gratitude are to our God daily given
For our Lord Christ who died and is risen.

But seek first his kingdom and his righteousness, and all
these things will be given to you as well.

MATTHEW 6:33

I LIVE ON

I WROTE THIS POEM ON THE SIXTH anniversary of the death of my twenty-five-year-old son, Whitner. It is written to give hope to others who have experienced great loss and heartbreak. It is written as an affirmation to know you can go on and live life, not as it was before, but as a new reality. You can still find joy cherishing each moment and each day as a blessed gift from God. You can live on.

*I have thankfulness though my
former life is no longer
I have peace though I live with
constant uncertainty*

263

I Live On

I can breathe though I thought I never could
I can laugh though I knew only tears
I can forget though I have experienced the unthinkable
I can live though I could hardly bear a day

I have love though my heart remains broken
I have joy though I carry great sorrow
I have hope though I know darkness and despair
I have faith though I have felt God's absence

I can rest though I have known constant tension
I can cope though I almost gave up
I can grow though my mind grew still and stagnant

I can flourish though my world once stopped

I have trust though I have been hurt and disappointed
I have gratitude though I know deep loss
I have thankfulness though my former life is no longer
I have peace though I live with constant uncertainty

I know my Redeemer because He has forgiven me
I know the Holy Spirit because He whispers to me
I know God because He never forsook me
I know His Son because He has died for me
So I live on.

Very truly I tell you, whoever hears my word and believes him who sent me has
eternal life and will not be judged but has crossed over from death to life.

JOHN 5:24

THANKFUL

I AM ESPECIALLY THANKFUL TO BE FREE to express my thoughts and to live the life I choose. I can know that no matter what happens, I will wake to a new day filled with hope and all kinds of possibilities. So I am thankful.

I stare at the setting sun and color-filled skies
I am thankful

Thankful

I freely speak my thoughts and ideas
I am thankful

I can achieve and be who I want to be
I am thankful

I have health and well-being
I am thankful

I awoke to a brand-new day
I am thankful

I share laughter with friends and family
I am thankful

I see life and miracles all around
I am thankful

I stare at the setting sun and
   color-filled skies

I am thankful

I smell the fragrance of jasmine
   in the wind
I am thankful

I hear music in the air
I am thankful

I can express my beliefs and faith
I am thankful

I feel God's love and faithfulness
I am thankful

I overflow with love and gratitude
I am thankful
I am thankful to be alive
I am thankful to be
I am thankful.

Give thanks to him and praise his name For the Lord is good and his love endures forever; his faithfulness continues through all generations.

PSALM 100:4–5

FEAR NOT

ON A TRIP TO PARIS, TO visit some dear friends, I was saddened by all the changes I saw. On street corners were police with guns, and the Eiffel Tower was fenced in with guards everywhere. There was a soccer game taking place, so there was high security. I have friends who will not travel to London or other cities in Europe for fear of terrorist attacks. In addition, the killings in Orlando, Brussels, and Paris have provoked fear in many around the world.

In light of this, I have written a poem about not giving in to fear, because with faith and trust in God our fear is removed. When we live in fear, we are allowing our earthly enemies to win and our greatest enemy, Satan, to win. When we trust in God, our fear vanishes, giving rise to freedom. This is freedom in Christ. When we have freedom in Christ, no one can really hurt us or provoke us to fear. Worst-case scenario? We die, but then we will be with our loving Savior. So fear not, my brothers and sisters.

*When worry and anxiety hold
you captive, fear not*

Fear Not

When the rain and clouds hover and persist,
  fear not
When worry and anxiety hold you captive,
  fear not
When your trust and belief waver, fear not
When you wonder if you can keep on breath-
  ing, fear not
When all those around you have lost control,
  fear not
When you find yourself in a bottomless abyss,
  fear not
When your trials and tribulations are never
  ceasing, fear not
When you keep trying but seem to always fail,
  fear not
When life seems hopeless with no promise,
  fear not
When all reason and logic don't give an
  answer, fear not

When life seems forever against you, fear not
When faulty thoughts overtake your mind,
  fear not
When you are approaching and facing death's
  door, fear not
When you don't know if you can make it
  another day, fear not
When the darkness of depression does not lift,
  fear not
When the oppression and abuse are too much
  to bear, fear not
When hurt leaves your heart in pieces, fear not
When loss and grief cause you endless pain,
  fear not
Since God is always with us, fear not
Since in God we trust, fear not
Since without fear, there is freedom, fear not
Since our freedom is in Christ, fear not.

Do not be afraid, for I am with you.

ISAIAH 43:5

WHEN THE IMPOSSIBLE OCCURS

WHEN THE HUMANLY IMPOSSIBLE OCCURS, THE only possibility becomes God.

Are you facing a problem or trial in your life that seems completely impossible to fix?

When it is humanly impossible, it is humanly impossible. The only possibility becomes God. It is supernatural, not of natural causes. Then why do we not readily accept God as the cause of the impossible? So, we should look to God in prayer and praise for those questions that seem to have no solution. With God all things are possible, even the impossible.

When the humanly impossible occurs,
the only possibility becomes God.

†

Jesus replied, "What is impossible with man is possible with God."

Luke 18:27

DEATH FALLS INTO DARKNESS

EATH IS THE DARK SPECTER THAT steals lives, but God robs death of its brief victory by receiving us into His loving arms. Death is defeated; its momentary victory is an illusion. God casts death back into the darkness. As John Donne wrote, "Death, be not proud, though some have called thee / Mighty and dreadful, for thou are not so. . . . One short sleep past, we wake eternally / And death shall be no more; Death, thou shalt die."

But, as death looms near it brings value and appreciation to life. Each second can then be seen as a treasured gift to be lived fully.

There is not a period, but only a brief pause
Darkness will go fleeting past with no deadly jaws

Death Falls Into Darkness

Death falls from the dark shadows
Lurking and creeping from the looming gallows

It is always a moment's breath near
It preys and feeds on our fear

Giving it power it does not deserve
It festers and thrives to disturb

Its victory is but a brief moment
Then God's triumph is its torment

No need to worry, no need to fret
Trust God; it will all be well, yet

We are just companions on a passenger train
But this brief respite does affect our heavenly gain

So on the day when we lay dying
There is no need for tears and crying

But what will it be that we have left
Love is what only matters and is kept

So let go of all else that the world holds
For every single mortal body will one day grow cold

In this life it's the intimate, loving connections
It's our honest self-inventory and reflections

The things that count give and send love
Other earthly things matter little up above

There is not a period, but only a brief pause
Darkness will go fleeting past with no
  deadly jaws

Death is not the final victor, but only the transmit-
  ting vector
God casts the final lethal demise of this sinister
  specter

A quiet moment's slumber, a dream away
To awake in this place where we will want to stay

So only a brief transition to our new eternal form
Our resurrected body will be our new norm

So death, hang your head low and bow down
Banish yourself to the darkness where you
  were found

Stand in exile as we receive our glory crowns
Then take yourself back to Hades underground

Death falls into the darkness, so your fate it does
  not cast
Mindfully live as it can be unexpected and fast

A frozen stilled heartbeat, then death is past
It is only a moment, a mere transition; it does
  not last.

When the perishable has been clothed with the imperishable, and the mortal with
immortality, then the saying that is written will come true: "Death has been swallowed
up in victory." "Where, O death, is your victory? Where, O death, is your sting?"

1 Corinthians 15:54–55

PUT YOUR TRUST IN GOD

AS WE FACE THE FUTURE WITH uncertainty, instead of giving in to fear, worry, anxiety, depression, and regret, let us place our trust in God. As a therapist and spiritual director, I find that many psychological problems, such as anxiety and depression, often originate from not trusting God. Fear and worry relate to not trusting God about our future. Regret over the past stems from not trusting God that our mistakes are forgiven and that our slates have been cleaned. So when we can truly trust God, we can be fully present to the present, where life takes place. By not ruminating on the past or fearing the future, we free ourselves from bondage of the thoughts that have held us captive. This is what it means to know true freedom in Christ. Let us live in that freedom now and into the future.

*As we face the future
with uncertainty . . .
Let us place our trust in God.*

HEAVEN

I HAVE TOLD ALL MY CHILDREN THAT I am "good to go" any time, that I have no fear of dying. It is all a win-win in living or in dying. I will either continue to be on earth with all of the people I love, or I will be in Heaven with all the other people I love and my Savior. It is sort of like Uncle Remus's Brer Rabbit saying, "Please don't throw me in the briar patch!" The briar patch to many would cause fear and pain, but Brer Rabbit yearned for it because it was his home. I would never choose death, but when it arrives, and it is my time, I will go with a peaceful smile on my face, as I will be returning home.

I have written much about death and dying, but what about Heaven? Here are my thoughts on what it will be like and what we have been promised in Scripture.

No more crying, no more tears
Vanished and gone are all our fears

Heaven

No more crying, no more tears
Vanished and gone are all our fears

Light shining all around
Darkness is nowhere to be found

Peace and love are the state
Never again do we have to wait

Our pleasure and wishes surround
Joy and sheer happiness abound

Laughter and frolic fill the day
Whatever we desire will be our way

Timelessness fades away the years

Health and vigor are what is here

Expansion and growth are the game
Life as we knew it will never be the same

Bonds and shackles are released
All sadness and sorrow have ceased

Only mere Heaven glimmers now confound
Then the trumpets and chorus will sound

But until then, Heaven must wait
Then on our last day we will cross through the gate

Where there are no more tears, no more crying
With Heaven's promise there is no fear in dying.

My Father's house has many rooms; if that were not so, would I have told
you that I am going there to prepare a place for you? And if I go and prepare a
place for you, I will come back and take you to be with me that you also may
be where I am. You know the way to the place where I am going.

JOHN 14:2–4

AN UNEXAMINED FAITH

AN UNEXAMINED FAITH IS NOT WORTH believing.
Socrates said an unexamined life is not worth living; I say an unexamined faith is not worth believing.

An examined faith has deep roots to anchor and a strong foundation to support it. It can withstand scrutiny, debate, and criticism—it is a faith that cannot be denied or denounced. An examined faith is a faith that evangelizes, making disciples of its believers.

An unexamined faith is not worth believing.

†

Therefore go and make disciples of all nations, baptizing them in the
name of the Father and of the Son and of the Holy Spirit.

MATTHEW 28:19

IN CLOSING . . .

BEING HUMAN IS ABOUT LOVING AND suffering and still maintaining hope. Life can be hard, and it can hurt. But despite that, always, always keep on loving, living, and believing.

I Believe

I believe in shooting stars that brighten the
 dark night
I believe they represent hope by shining their light

I believe in asking and knowing the reasons
I believe life always changes as the seasons

I believe in things I cannot see
I believe the answers may be mystery

I believe in keeping friendships, never
 saying goodbyes
I believe simple joy may be found in sunshine
 and blue skies

I believe in life, that it is what you make it
I believe in grasping for the highest rung
 and taking it

I believe in aiming for the brightest star
I believe no matter how hard or how far

I believe in life as an exciting adventure to
 be fully lived
I believe my heart and soul I must fully give

I believe in positivity, to be an optimist
I believe loving first no matter what the risk

I believe in singing my true heart's song
I believe it is never too late to right a wrong

I believe in feeling but not focusing on my sorrow
I believe life is to be lived as if there is no tomorrow

I believe in excelling at my strengths, so I can soar
I believe letting my heart and voice roar

I believe in letting my heart and imagination
 run wild
I believe my inner self there still remains a
 playful, innocent child

I believe in love even when I hurt and fall
I believe love's magic when it calls

I believe in the hope of each new day
I believe it holds promise of a brand-new way

I believe in butterfly kisses
I believe true love is still realistic

I believe in dreams being my voice
I believe happiness is my choice

I believe in myself that I will safely land
I believe if I think I can, I can

I believe in miracles and dreams coming true
I believe joy and peace will ensue

I believe in taking risks even if I lose
I believe my life's passions must be pursued

I believe in the sun even with clouds and rain
I believe all people should be respected and treated
 the same

I believe in love even if my heart has been broken
 and torn

I believe life is a mystical and spiritual sojourn

I believe in kindness and always caring
I believe it's all about giving and sharing

I believe in one look, one word can make
  a difference
I believe life can be changed in that instant

I believe in God's love and His plans
I believe I am always in my Master's loving hands

I believe in the end everything will be God's say
I believe Him, so I will always trust His way

I believe in giving love, not keeping it within
I believe Jesus's blood righted all my sins

I believe in God and His hope to prosper me
I believe Christ's love has set me free

I believe in Jesus that His face I will one day see
I believe I will go on living and loving forever,
  in eternity

I believe.

May the God of hope fill you with all joy and peace as you trust in him, so that you
may overflow with hope by the power of the Holy Spirit.

ROMANS 15:13

AUTHOR'S NOTE

AS A THERAPIST, I SEE THAT most of us have a core issue that motivates and drives us. It may drive us to have a need met, or it may block us from getting what we want.

More often than not, I find that our core issue has to do with a feeling of unworthiness or a belief that we're unlovable. *Do I feel worthy or good enough? Do I feel lovable?* My own issue revolves around a fear of abandonment, but I recognize that at its core it is a feeling of not being good enough. I lived a long time thinking that I wouldn't be abandoned if I was perfect, and if I was perfect, I would be good enough or worthy.

On the surface, I may appear confident. But surface appearances aren't always true. Childhood feelings of abandonment had always led me to try to be perfect. My parents divorced by the time I was five, and my mother was left with the sole responsibility of raising me. My dad abused alcohol, which in hindsight I believe was actually self-medication for his depression. He was, by all accounts, an alcoholic who never sought treatment. I knew I was very loved by my mother and by my father, as much as he could show love.

My mother worked full time and would come home each day extremely tired. If I misbehaved, in her desperation, she would threaten me to keep me in line. The message I received as a young girl was that I needed to be perfect so I wouldn't be abandoned or rejected. I thought that if I misbehaved or was anything less than perfect, my mother would send me to live with my alcoholic father.

My father loved me. However, he left me as a young child. My mother loved me as she cared for me, but in her fatigue, at times she would threaten to send me away, aggravating my fear of abandonment. Growing up with these impressions affected the kind of adult I became. My fear of abandonment led me to try very hard to be perfect and good in *all* the parts of my life. I thought if I was the problem solver, the helper, the one you could depend on to always be there, people would need me. I would make myself essential to people so that I couldn't possibly be discarded or left out. On the other hand, if people didn't need me, I considered them not safe, and I pushed them away.

Finding Freedom through God's Love

What I have found through my life's journey is that it becomes depleting and exhausting to try to be essential. It leads to unhealthy, codependent relationships. I realized at some point that I couldn't please everyone all the time and that I would never be perfect. But because of my growing faith, I knew God loved and accepted me just as I was: with all my faults and imperfections. He created me as I was, and He saw the true me beneath the exterior.

This epiphany in my relationship with the Lord has led me to freedom. It has enabled me to be transparent, open, and honest about the person I am with all my faults, mistakes, and sins. It has enabled me to share my life experiences, my deeply personal poetry, and my relationship with God in my efforts to help others. The solution, I believe, to all our woundedness and brokenness in life is always found in God's love for us. It has been the answer for me. My prayer is that my poetry, even if in some small way, brings each of you some comfort, a little encouragement and inspiration, the recognition of hope in your life, and a step closer to healing.

Now the Lord is the Spirit, and where the Spirit of the Lord is, there is freedom.

2 CORINTHIANS 3:17

ACKNOWLEDGMENTS

I FIRST WOULD LIKE TO THANK MY social media and blog followers of Healing Presence Ministry who, through their words of encouragement and enjoyment and appreciation of my poetry and writings, inspired me to take the step to publish.

I want to extend my deepest appreciation to Britt in her devotion to my ministry and in her diligent help in compiling this book for publication.

With much gratitude to my husband for his never-failing support of my poetry and writings. Without it, my work would have had little exposure and may never have been published.

Many thanks to a special friend who first encouraged me to muster the courage to share my poetry publicly.

Most importantly, in the publication of this book, I want to thank my Greenleaf editors and the staff for their impeccable and visionary work in helping me improve my first published work, making it even more than I ever anticipated in content and quality.

And, of course, with an overflowing and grateful heart, I give thanks to God, His Son, and the Holy Spirit for being the Ones who actually inspire my poetry and writings. To them, I give all the glory and praise.

ADDITIONAL VERSES

Preface

The Source   xiii

"For I know the plans I have for you," declares the Lord, "plans to prosper you and not to harm you, plans to give you hope and a future." (Jeremiah 29:11)

Ask and it will be given to you; seek and you will find; knock and the door will be opened to you. For everyone who asks receives; the one who seeks finds; and to the one who knocks, the door will be opened. (Matthew 7:7–8)

For since the creation of the world God's invisible qualities—his eternal power and divine nature—have been clearly seen, being understood from what has been made, so that people are without excuse. (Romans 1:20)

Introduction

On Being Human   2

And he said: "Truly I tell you, unless you change and become like little children, you will never enter the kingdom of heaven." (Matthew 18:3)

God did this so that they would seek him and perhaps reach out for him and find him, though he is not far from any one of us. "For in him we live and move and have our being." As some of your own poets have said, "We are his offspring." (Acts 17:27–28)

Part One: Human Love

Matters of the Heart   9

Create in me a pure heart, O God, and renew a steadfast spirit within me. (Psalm 51:10)

My flesh and my heart may fail, but God is the strength of my heart and my portion forever. (Psalm 73:26)

From that time on Jesus began to explain to his disciples that he must go to Jerusalem and suffer many things at the hands of the elders, the chief priests and the teachers of the law, and that he must be killed and on the third day be raised to life. (Matthew 16:21)

To Be Loved   12

Give thanks to the Lord, for he is good; his love endures forever. (1 Chronicles 16:34)

But you, Lord, are a compassionate and gracious God, slow to anger, abounding in love and faithfulness. (Psalm 86:15)

But God demonstrates his own love for us in this: While we were still sinners, Christ died for us. (Romans 5:8)

And over all these virtues put on love, which binds them all together in perfect unity. (Colossians 3:14)

You Walked Away   15

No one will be able to stand against you all the days of your life. As I was with Moses, so I will be with you; I will never leave you nor forsake you. (Joshua 1:5)

Whoever dwells in the shelter of the Most High will rest in the shadow of the Almighty. I will say of the Lord, "He is my refuge and my fortress, my God, in whom I trust." . . . He will cover you with his feathers, and under his wings you will find refuge; his faithfulness will be your shield and rampart. (Psalm 91:1–2, 4)

I lift my eyes to the mountains—where does my help come from? My help comes from the Lord, the Maker of heaven and earth. He will not let your foot slip—he who watches over you will not slumber; indeed, he who watches over Israel will neither slumber nor sleep. The Lord watches over you—the Lord is your shade at your right hand; the sun will not harm you by day, nor the moon by night. The Lord will keep you from all harm—he will watch over your life; the Lord will watch over your coming and going both now and forevermore. (Psalm 121:1–8)

Did I Know? 18

For no word from God will ever fail. (Luke 1:37)

We know that the law is spiritual; but I am unspiritual, sold as a slave to sin. I do not understand what I do. For what I want to do I do not do, but what I hate I do. And if I do what I do not want to do, I agree that the law is good. As it is, it is no longer I myself who do it, but it is sin living in me. For I know that good itself does not dwell in me, that is, in my sinful nature. For I have the desire to do what is good, but I cannot carry it out. For I do not do the good I want to do, but the evil I do not want to do—this I keep on doing. Now if I do what I do not want to do, it is no longer I who do it, but it is sin living in me that does it.

So I find this law at work: Although I want to do good, evil is right there with me. For in my inner being I delight in God's law; but I see another law at work in me, waging war against the law of my mind and making me a prisoner of the law of sin at work within me. What a wretched man I am! Who will rescue me from this body that is subject to death? Thanks be to God, who delivers me through Jesus Christ our Lord!

So then, I myself in my mind am a slave to God's law, but in my sinful nature a slave to the law of sin. (Romans 7:14–25)

I can do all this through him who gives me strength. (Philippians 4:13)

Both Sides of Love 21

Praise the Lord. Give thanks to the Lord, for he is good; his love endures forever. (Psalm 106:1)

And now these three remain: faith, hope and love. But the greatest of these is love. (1 Corinthians 13:13)

Evergreen Evermore 24

Jesus looked at them and said, "With man this is impossible, but with God all things are possible." (Matthew 19:26)

Whoever does not love does not know God, because God is love. (1 John 4:8)

On Marriage 27

It is God who arms me with strength and keeps my way secure. He makes my feet like the feet of a deer; he causes me to stand on the heights. (Psalm 18:32–33)

Therefore everyone who hears these words of mine and puts them into practice is like a wise man who built his house on the rock. The rain came down, the streams rose, and the winds blew and beat against that house; yet it did not fall, because it had its foundation on the rock. But everyone who hears these words of mine and does not put them into practice is like a foolish man who built his house on sand. The rain came down, the streams rose, and the winds blew and beat against that house, and it fell with a great crash. (Matthew 7:24–27)

Love must be sincere. Hate what is evil; cling to what is good. Be devoted to one another in love. Honor one another above yourselves. Never be lacking in zeal, but keep your spiritual fervor, serving the Lord. Be joyful in hope, patient in affliction, faithful in prayer. Share with the Lord's people who are in need. Practice hospitality.

Bless those who persecute you; bless and do not curse. Rejoice with those who rejoice; mourn with those who mourn. Live in harmony with one another. Do not be proud, but be willing to associate with people of low position. (Romans 12:9–16)

Forgiveness   30

But if you do not forgive others their sins, your Father will not forgive your sins. (Matthew 6:15)

But to you who are listening I say: Love your enemies, do good to those who hate you. (Luke 6:27)

Bear with each other and forgive one another if any of you has a grievance against someone. Forgive as the Lord forgave you. (Colossians 3:13)

Therefore confess your sins to each other and pray for each other so that you may be healed. The prayer of a righteous person is powerful and effective. (James 5:16)

Reflections in a Mirrored Glass   33

For now we see only a reflection as in a mirror; then we shall see face to face. Now I know in part; then I shall know fully, even as I am fully known. (1 Corinthians 13:12)

And we all, who with unveiled faces contemplate the Lord's glory, are being transformed into his image with ever-increasing glory, which comes from the Lord, who is the Spirit. (2 Corinthians 3:18)

And so we know and rely on the love God has for us. God is love. Whoever lives in love lives in God, and God in them. (1 John 4:16)

House of the Soul   36

I praise you because I am fearfully and wonderfully made; your works are wonderful, I know that full well. (Psalm 139:14)

Therefore we are always confident and know that as long as we are at home in the

body we are away from the Lord. For we live by faith, not by sight. We are confident, I say, and would prefer to be away from the body and at home with the Lord.
(2 Corinthians 5:6–8)

Connection   39

So God created mankind in his own image, in the image of God he created them; male and female he created them. (Genesis 1:27)

And let us consider how we may spur one another on toward love and good deeds, not giving up meeting together, as some are in the habit of doing, but encouraging one another—and all the more as you see the Day approaching. (Hebrews 10:24–25)

This Thing Called Love   42

My command is this: Love each other as I have loved you. (John 15:12)

Love is patient, love is kind. It does not envy, it does not boast, it is not proud. It does not dishonor others, it is not self-seeking, it is not easily angered, it keeps no record of wrongs. Love does not delight in evil but rejoices with the truth. It always protects, always trusts, always hopes, always perseveres. Love never fails.
(1 Corinthians 13:4–8)

She   45

Have I not commanded you? Be strong and courageous. Do not be afraid; do not be discouraged, for the Lord your God will be with you wherever you go. (Joshua 1:9)

God is within her, she will not fall.
(Psalm 46:5)

She is clothed with strength and dignity; she can laugh at the days to come. She speaks with wisdom, and faithful instruction is on her tongue. She watches over the affairs of her household and does not eat the bread of idleness. Her children arise and call her blessed; her husband also, and he praises her: "Many women do noble things, but you surpass them all." Charm is deceptive, and beauty is fleeting; but a woman who fears the Lord is to be praised.
(Proverbs 31:25–30)

God's Muse   48

Those who know your name trust in you, for you, Lord, have never forsaken those who seek you. (Psalm 9:10)

Some trust in chariots and some in horses, but we trust in the name of the Lord our God. (Psalm 20:7)

Be Kind 51

Be completely humble and gentle; be patient, bearing with one another in love. Make every effort to keep the unity of the Spirit through the bond of peace.
(Ephesians 4:2–3)

Dear friends, let us love one another, for love comes from God. Everyone who loves has been born of God and knows God. Whoever does not love does not know God, because God is love. This is how God showed his love among us: He sent his one and only Son into the world that we might live through him. (1 John 4:7–9)

Repentance 54

In repentance and rest is your salvation, in quietness and trust is your strength.
(Isaiah 30:15)

From that time on Jesus began to preach, "Repent, for the kingdom of heaven has come near." (Matthew 4:17)

Part Two: God's Love

The Divine Paradox 59

"For I know the plans I have for you," declares the Lord, "plans to prosper you and not to harm you, plans to give you hope and a future." (Jeremiah 29:11)

And we know that in all things God works for the good of those who love him, who have been called according to his purpose. (Romans 8:28)

Beloved 62

Yet you, Lord, are our Father. We are the clay, you are the potter; we are all the work of your hand. (Isaiah 64:8)

See what great love the Father has lavished on us, that we should be called children of God! And that is what we are! The reason the world does not know us is that it did not know him. (1 John 3:1)

Home 65

"For in him we live and move and have our being." As some of your own poets have said, "We are his offspring." (Acts 17:28)

For I am convinced that neither death nor life, neither angels nor demons, neither the present nor the future, nor any powers, neither height nor depth, nor anything else in all creation, will be able to separate us from the love of God that is in Christ Jesus our Lord. (Romans 8:38–39)

In This Holy Place 68

My heart says of you, "Seek his face!" Your face, Lord, I will seek. (Psalm 27:8)

My dear children, I write this to you so that you will not sin. But if anybody does sin, we have an advocate with the Father—Jesus Christ, the Righteous One. He is the atoning sacrifice for our sins, and not only for ours but also for the sins of the whole world. (1 John 2:1–2)

Waiting Is a God Game   71

So Jacob served seven years to get Rachel, but they seemed like only a few days to him because of his love for her. (Genesis 29:20)

Be still before the Lord and wait patiently for him; do not fret when people succeed in their ways, when they carry out their wicked schemes. (Psalm 37:7)

The Prayer of the Wandering Sheep   74

The Lord is my shepherd, I lack nothing. He makes me lie down in green pastures, he leads me beside quiet waters, he refreshes my soul. He guides me along the right paths for his name's sake. (Psalm 23:1–3)

I am the good shepherd; I know my sheep and my sheep know me—just as the Father knows me and I know the Father—and I lay down my life for the sheep.
(John 10:14–15)

Consequences   77

For the wages of sin is death, but the gift of God is eternal life in Christ Jesus our Lord. (Romans 6:23)

Do not be deceived: God cannot be mocked. A man reaps what he sows. Whoever sows to please their flesh, from the flesh will reap destruction; whoever sows to please the Spirit, from the Spirit will reap eternal life. (Galatians 6:7–8)

Redemption   80

I know that my redeemer lives, and that in the end he will stand on the earth. (Job 19:25)

And we know that in all things God works for the good of those who love him, who have been called according to his purpose. (Romans 8:28)

However, as it is written: "What no eye has seen, what no ear has heard, and what no human mind has conceived"—the things God has prepared for those who love him. (1 Corinthians 2:9)

Where Is God?   83

You make known to me the path of life; you will fill me with joy in your presence, with eternal pleasures at your right hand. (Psalm 16:11)

I will give thanks to you, Lord, with all my heart; I will tell of all your wonderful deeds. (Psalm 9:1)

And the Cows Lay Down   86

Jesus said, "Father, forgive them, for they do not know what they are doing." (Luke 23:34)

For since the creation of the world God's invisible qualities—his eternal power and divine nature—have been clearly seen, being understood from what has been made, so that people are without excuse. (Romans 1:20)

The Gift of Christmas   89

The Word became flesh and made his dwelling among us. We have seen his glory, the glory of the one and only Son, who came from the Father, full of grace and truth. (John 1:14)

For God so loved the world that he gave his one and only Son, that whoever believes in him shall not perish but have eternal life. (John 3:16)

He Is Risen   92

Very truly I tell you, whoever hears my word and believes him who sent me has eternal life and will not be judged but has crossed over from death to life. (John 5:24)

I am the living bread that came down from heaven. Whoever eats this bread will live forever. This bread is my flesh, which I will give for the life of the world. (John 6:51)

Do not let your hearts be troubled. You believe in God; believe also in me. My Father's house has many rooms; if that were not so, would I have told you that I am going there to prepare a place for you? And if I go and prepare a place for you, I will come back and take you to be with me that you also may be where I am. You know the way to the place where I am going. (John 14:1–4)

Jesus answered, "I am the way and the truth and the life. No one comes to the Father except through me. . . . But the Advocate, the Holy Spirit, whom the Father will send in my name, will teach you all things and will remind you of everything I have said to you. Peace I leave with you; my peace I give you. I do not give to you as the world gives. Do not let your hearts be troubled and do not be afraid." (John 14:6, 26–27)

No, the Father himself loves you because you have loved me and have believed that I came from God. I came from the Father and entered the world; now I am leaving the world and going back to the Father. (John 16:27–28)

I am the Alpha and the Omega, the First and the Last, the Beginning and the End. (Revelation 22:13)

Love's Wellspring   95

My command is this: Love each other as I have loved you. (John 15:12)

And over all these virtues put on love, which binds them all together in perfect unity. (Colossians 3:14)

Time to Timeless   98

Show me, Lord, my life's end and the number of my days; let me know how fleeting my life is. You have made my days a mere handbreadth; the span of my years is as nothing before you. Everyone is but a breath, even those who seem secure. Surely everyone goes around like a mere phantom; in vain they rush about, heaping up wealth without knowing whose it will finally be. But now, Lord, what do I look for? My hope is in you. (Psalm 39:4–7)

Jesus Christ is the same yesterday and today and forever. (Hebrews 13:8)

This is love: not that we loved God, but that he loved us and sent his Son as an atoning sacrifice for our sins. . . . And so we know and rely on the love God has for us. God is love. Whoever lives in love lives in God, and God in them. (1 John 4:10, 16)

A Sinner's Song   101

For all have sinned and fall short of the glory of God. (Romans 3:23)

But if we walk in the light, as he is in the light, we have fellowship with one another, and the blood of Jesus, his Son, purifies us from all sin. If we claim to be without sin, we deceive ourselves and the truth is not in us. If we confess our sins, he is faithful and just and will forgive us our sins and purify us from all unrighteousness. (1 John 1:7–9)

He   104

Hear, O Israel: The Lord our God, the Lord is one. (Deuteronomy 6:4)

The Lord bless you and keep you; the Lord make his face shine on you and be gracious to you; the Lord turn his face toward you and give you peace. (Numbers 6:24–26)

The Lord watches over you—the Lord is your shade at your right hand; the sun will not harm you by day, nor the moon by night. The Lord will keep you from all harm—he will watch over your life; the Lord will watch over your coming and going both now and forevermore. (Psalm 121:5–8)

The Call of the Sea   107

I will remember my covenant between me and you and all living creatures of every kind. Never again will the waters become a flood to destroy all life. (Genesis 9:15)

I the Lord do not change. So you, the descendants of Jacob, are not destroyed. (Malachi 3:6)

Part Three: Suffering

Understanding Suffering   110

Yet man is born to trouble as surely as sparks fly upward. (Job 5:7)

He who dwells in the shelter of the Most High will rest in the shadow of the Almighty. (Psalm 91:1)

I have fought the good fight, I have finished the race, I have kept the faith. Now there is in store for me the crown of righteousness, which the Lord, the righteous Judge, will award to me on that day—and not only to me, but also to all who have longed for his appearing. (2 Timothy 4:7–8)

Sorrow to Song   115

Jesus looked at them and said, "With man this is impossible, but with God all things are possible." (Matthew 19:26)

For we live by faith, not by sight. (2 Corinthians 5:7)

The Way Back   118

Enter through the narrow gate. For wide is the gate and broad is the road that leads to destruction, and many enter through it. But small is the gate and narrow the road that leads to life, and only a few find it. (Matthew 7:13–14)

For no word from God will ever fail. (Luke 1:37)

If God is for us, who can be against us? He who did not spare his own Son, but gave him up for us all—how will he not also, along with him, graciously give us all things? (Romans 8:31–32)

Do not be anxious about anything, but in every situation, by prayer and petition, with thanksgiving, present your requests to God. And the peace of God, which transcends all understanding, will guard your hearts and your minds in Christ Jesus. (Philippians 4:6–7)

Into the Light   121

You, Lord, keep my lamp burning; my God turns my darkness into light. (Psalm 18:28)

Because of the tender mercy of our God, by which the rising sun will come to us from heaven to shine on those living in darkness and in the shadow of death, to guide our feet into the path of peace. (Luke 1:78–79)

When Jesus spoke again to the people, he said, "I am the light of the world. Whoever follows me will never walk in darkness, but will have the light of life." (John 8:12)

Then Jesus told them, "You are going to have the light just a little while longer. Walk while you have the light, before darkness overtakes you. Whoever walks in the dark does not know where they are going. Believe in the light while you have the light, so that you may become children of light." When he had finished speaking, Jesus left and hid himself from them.
(John 12:35–36)

For he has rescued us from the dominion of darkness and brought us into the kingdom of the Son he loves. (Colossians 1:13)

If I Can Just Keep On Breathing   124

Hear, Lord, and be merciful to me; Lord, be my help. You turned my wailing into dancing; you removed my sackcloth and clothed me with joy, that my heart may sing your praises and not be silent. Lord my God, I will praise you forever. (Psalm 30:10–12)

I call on the Lord in my distress, and he answers me. (Psalm 120:1)

I lift up my eyes to the mountains—where does my help come from? My help comes from the Lord, the Maker of heaven and earth. (Psalm 121:1–2)

The Spirit of the Sovereign Lord is on me, because the Lord has anointed me to proclaim good news to the poor. He has sent me to bind up the brokenhearted, to proclaim freedom for the captives and release from darkness for the prisoners, to proclaim the year of the Lord's favor and the day of vengeance of our God, to comfort all who mourn, and provide for those who grieve in Zion—to bestow on them a crown of beauty instead of ashes, the oil of joy instead of mourning, and a garment of praise instead of a spirit of despair. They will be called oaks of righteousness, a planting of the Lord for the display of his splendor. (Isaiah 61:1–3)

I Stumble and Fall Down   128

I will heal their waywardness and love them freely, for my anger has turned away from them. (Hosea 14:4)

"He himself bore our sins" in his body on the cross, so that we might die to sins and live for righteousness; "by his wounds you have been healed." (1 Peter 2:24)

Do You Really See Me?   131

Blessed are those who have regard for the weak; the Lord delivers them in times of trouble. The Lord protects and preserves them—they are counted among the blessed in the land—he does not give them over to the desire of their foes. (Psalm 41:1–2)

It is a sin to despise one's neighbor, but blessed is the one who is kind to the needy. (Proverbs 14:21)

The King will reply, "Truly I tell you, whatever you did for one of the least of these brothers and sisters of mine, you did for me." (Matthew 25:40)

No One Knows   134

Be strong and courageous. Do not be afraid or terrified because of them, for the Lord your God goes with you; he will never leave you nor forsake you. (Deuteronomy 31:6)

Have I not commanded you? Be strong and courageous. Do not be afraid; do not be discouraged, for the Lord your God will be with you wherever you go. (Joshua 1:9)

But God demonstrates his own love for us in this: While we were still sinners, Christ died for us. (Romans 5:8)

We live by faith, not by sight. (2 Corinthians 5:7)

For everyone born of God overcomes the world. This is the victory that has overcome the world, even our faith. (1 John 5:4)

When You Don't Understand   137

He replied, "You of little faith, why are you so afraid?" Then he got up and rebuked the winds and the waves, and it was completely calm. (Matthew 8:26)

I have fought the good fight, I have finished the race, I have kept the faith. Now there is in store for me the crown of righteousness, which the Lord, the righteous Judge, will award to me on that day. (2 Timothy 4:7–8)

Living in the Valleys of Life   138

"Though the mountains be shaken and the hills be removed, yet my unfailing love for you will not be shaken nor my covenant of peace be removed," says the Lord, who has compassion on you. (Isaiah 54:10)

I am the good shepherd. The good shepherd lays down his life for the sheep. (John 10:11)

You Came with Angel's Wings   142

The Lord is good to all; he has compassion on all he has made. (Psalm 145:9)

The wolf will live with the lamb, the leopard will lie down with the goat, the calf and the lion and the yearling together; and a

little child will lead them. . . . They will nei-
ther harm nor destroy on my holy moun-
tain, for the earth will be filled with the
knowledge of the Lord as the waters cover
the sea. (Isaiah 11:6, 9)

The Long Goodbye   145

In the same way, the Spirit helps us in our
weakness. We do not know what we ought
to pray for, but the Spirit himself intercedes
for us through wordless groans.
(Romans 8:26)

A time to weep and a time to laugh, a time
to mourn and a time to dance.
(Ecclesiastes 3:4)

And the God of all grace, who called you
to his eternal glory in Christ, after you have
suffered a little while, will himself restore
you and make you strong, firm and stead-
fast. To him be the power for ever and ever.
Amen. (1 Peter 5:10–11)

When It's Over   148

Show me, Lord, my life's end and the num-
ber of my days; let me know how fleet-
ing my life is. You have made my days a
mere handbreadth; the span of my years is
as nothing before you. Everyone is but a
breath, even those who seem secure. Surely
everyone goes around like a mere phantom;
in vain they rush about, heaping up wealth
without knowing whose it will finally be.

But now, Lord, what do I look for? My
hope is in you. (Psalm 39:4–7)

The life of mortals is like grass, they flour-
ish like a flower of the field; the wind blows
over it and it is gone, and its place remem-
bers it no more. (Psalm 103:15–16)

A voice says, "Cry out." And I said, "What
shall I cry?" "All people are like grass, and
all their faithfulness is like the flowers of the
field. The grass withers and the flowers fall,
because the breath of the Lord blows on
them. Surely the people are grass. The grass
withers and the flowers fall, but the word of
our God endures forever." (Isaiah 40:6–8)

A Reflection on the Death of my
Son: A Lament of Promise 150

For the Lord is good and his love endures
forever; his faithfulness continues through
all generations. (Psalm 100:5)

My days are like the evening shadow; I wither
away like grass. But you, Lord, sit enthroned
forever; your renown endures through all
generations. You will rise and have compas-
sion on Zion. (Psalm 102:11–13)

He heals the brokenhearted and binds up
their wounds. (Psalm 147:3)

Blessed are those who mourn, for they will
be comforted. (Matthew 5:4)

The Language of Loss   157

But you, God, see the trouble of the afflicted; you consider their grief and take it in hand. The victims commit themselves to you; you are the helper of the fatherless. (Psalm 10:14)

For our light and momentary troubles are achieving for us an eternal glory that far outweighs them all. So we fix our eyes not on what is seen, but on what is unseen, since what is seen is temporary, but what is unseen is eternal. (2 Corinthians 4:17–18)

Choices   160

No one can serve two masters. Either you will hate the one and love the other, or you will be devoted to the one and despise the other. (Matthew 6:24)

"But what about you?" he asked. "Who do you say I am?"

Simon Peter answered, "You are the Messiah, the Son of the living God." (Matthew 16:15–16)

Betrayal   163

For this reason a man will leave his father and mother and be united to his wife, and the two will become one flesh. (Ephesians 5:31)

Bear with each other and forgive one another if any of you has a grievance against someone. Forgive as the Lord forgave you. (Colossians 3:13)

If we confess our sins, he is faithful and just and will forgive us our sins and purify us from all unrighteousness. (1 John 1:9)

Only with God   166

Jesus looked at them and said, "With man this is impossible, but not with God; all things are possible with God." (Mark 10:27)

For no word from God will ever fail. (Luke 1:37)

Trust God into the Abyss   169

Look to the Lord and his strength; seek his face always. (1 Chronicles 16:11)

For the word of the Lord is right and true; he is faithful in all he does. The Lord loves righteousness and justice; the earth is full of his unfailing love. By the word of the Lord the heavens were made, their starry host by the breath of his mouth. (Psalm 33:4–6)

"I am the Alpha and the Omega," says the Lord God, "who is, and who was, and who is to come, the Almighty." (Revelation 1:8)

The Past Is Never Very Far Away   172

Praise the Lord, my soul, and forget not all his benefits—who forgives all your sins and heals all your diseases. (Psalm 103:2–3)

So do not fear, for I am with you; do not be dismayed, for I am your God. I will strengthen you and help you; I will uphold you with my righteous right hand. (Isaiah 41:10)

Ode to Heroin   176

As for God, his way is perfect: The Lord's word is flawless; he shields all who take refuge in him. (2 Samuel 22:31)

Cast your cares on the Lord and he will sustain you; he will never let the righteous be shaken. (Psalm 55:22)

But the Lord is faithful, and he will strengthen you and protect you from the evil one. (2 Thessalonians 3:3)

Ndutu   179

Your kingdom come, your will be done, on earth as it is in heaven. (Matthew 6:10)

For in him all things were created: things in heaven and on earth, visible and invisible, whether thrones or powers or rulers or authorities; all things have been created through him and for him. He is before all things, and in him all things hold together. (Colossians 1:16–17)

The Question of Hell   180

And so we know and rely on the love God has for us. God is love. Whoever lives in love lives in God, and God in them. (1 John 4:16)

He will wipe every tear from their eyes. There will be no more death or mourning or crying or pain, for the old order of things has passed away. (Revelation 21:4)

More on the Question of Hell   183

Listen, I tell you a mystery: We will not all sleep, but we will all be changed—in a flash, in the twinkling of an eye, at the last trumpet. For the trumpet will sound, the dead will be raised imperishable, and we will be changed. For the perishable must clothe itself with the imperishable, and the mortal with immortality. When the perishable has been clothed with the imperishable, and the mortal with immortality, then the saying that is written will come true: "Death has been swallowed up in victory." (1 Corinthians 15:51–54)

But the cowardly, the unbelieving, the vile, the murderers, the sexually immoral, those who practice magic arts, the idolaters and all liars—they will be consigned to the fiery lake of burning sulfur. This is the second death. (Revelation 21:8)

And God Cried   188

Therefore go and make disciples of all nations, baptizing them in the name of the Father and of the Son and of the Holy Spirit. (Matthew 28:19)

My command is this: Love each other as I have loved you. (John 15:12)

This Side of Heaven   192

The Lord makes firm the steps of the one who delights in him; though he may stumble, he will not fall, for the Lord upholds him with his hand. (Psalm 37:23–24)

For I am the Lord your God who takes hold of your right hand and says to you, Do not fear; I will help you. (Isaiah 41:13)

Walk On   196

Are not two sparrows sold for a penny? Yet not one of them will fall to the ground outside your Father's care. (Matthew 10:29)

Now there is in store for me the crown of righteousness, which the Lord, the righteous Judge, will award to me on that day—and not only to me, but also to all who have longed for his appearing. (2 Timothy 4:8)

Behind the Smile   200

But those who hope in the Lord will renew their strength. They will soar on wings like eagles; they will run and not grow weary, they will walk and not be faint. (Isaiah 40:31)

The Sovereign Lord is my strength; he makes my feet like the feet of a deer, he enables me to tread on the heights. (Habakkuk 3:19)

Tears Beneath   203

You are my hiding place; you will protect me from trouble and surround me with songs of deliverance. (Psalm 32:7)

The Lord is close to the brokenhearted and saves those who are crushed in spirit. (Psalm 34:18)

He replied, "Because you have so little faith. Truly I tell you, if you have faith as small as a mustard seed, you can say to this mountain, 'Move from here to there,' and it will move. Nothing will be impossible for you." (Matthew 17:20–21)

Everything is possible for one who believes. (Mark 9:23)

What, then, shall we say in response to these things? If God is for us, who can be against us? He who did not spare his own Son, but gave him up for us all—how will he not also, along with him, graciously give us all things? Who will bring any charge against those whom God has chosen? It is God who justifies. Who then is the one who condemns? No one. Christ Jesus who died—more than that, who was raised to life—is at the right hand of God and is also interceding for us. Who shall separate us from the love of Christ? Shall trouble or hardship or persecution or famine or nakedness or danger or sword? As it is written: "For your sake we face death all day long; we are considered as sheep to be slaughtered."

No, in all these things we are more than conquerors through him who loved us. For I am convinced that neither death nor life, neither angels nor demons, neither the present nor the future, nor any powers, neither height nor depth, nor anything else in all creation, will be able to separate us from the love of God that is in Christ Jesus our Lord. (Romans 8:31–39)

A Season for All Things   206

But blessed is the one who trusts in the Lord, whose confidence is in him. They will be like a tree planted by the water that sends out its roots by the stream. It does not fear when heat comes; its leaves are always green. It has no worries in a year of drought and never fails to bear fruit.
(Jeremiah 17:7–8)

Do not let your hearts be troubled. You believe in God; believe also in me.
(John 14:1)

Part Four: Hope
New Beginnings   211

The Lord has done it this very day; let us rejoice today and be glad. (Psalm 118:24)

For everyone born of God overcomes the world. This is the victory that has overcome the world, even our faith. Who is it that overcomes the world? Only the one who believes that Jesus is the Son of God. (1 John 5:4–5)

Be Still   212

The Lord is near to all who call on him, to all who call on him in truth. (Psalm 145:18)
God did this so that they would seek him and perhaps reach out for him and find him, though he is not far from any one of us. (Acts 17:27)

A Moment in Time   216

Surely everyone goes around like a mere phantom; in vain they rush about, heaping up wealth without knowing whose it will finally be. But now, Lord, what do I look for? My hope is in you. (Psalm 39:6–7)

Teach us to number our days, that we may gain a heart of wisdom. (Psalm 90:12)

Gratitude   219

Shout for joy to the Lord, all the earth. Worship the Lord with gladness; come before him with joyful songs. Know that the Lord is God. It is he who made us, and we are his; we are his people, the sheep of his pasture. Enter his gates with thanksgiving and his courts with praise; give thanks to him and praise his name. For the Lord is good and his love endures forever; his faithfulness continues through all generations. (Psalm 100:1–5)

Give thanks to the God of heaven. His love endures forever. (Psalm 136:26)

Give thanks in all circumstances; for this is God's will for you in Christ Jesus. (1 Thessalonians 5:18)

Peace   222

Peace I leave with you; my peace I give you. I do not give to you as the world gives. Do not let your hearts be troubled and do not be afraid. (John 14:27)

I have told you these things, so that in me you may have peace. In this world you will have trouble. But take heart! I have overcome the world. (John 16:33)

Here I am! I stand at the door and knock. If anyone hears my voice and opens the door, I will come in and eat with that person, and they with me. (Revelation 3:20)

What If?   225

No one will be able to stand against you; all the days of your life. As I was with Moses, so I will be with you; I will never leave you nor forsake you. (Joshua 1:5)

Keep your lives free from the love of money and be content with what you have, because God has said, "Never will I leave you; never will I forsake you." (Hebrews 13:5)

Rise Up   228

When I am afraid, I put my trust in you. In God, whose word I praise—in God I trust and am not afraid. What can mere mortals do to me? (Psalm 56:3–4)

And provide for those who grieve in Zion— to bestow on them a crown of beauty instead of ashes, the oil of joy instead of mourning, and a garment of praise instead of a spirit of despair. (Isaiah 61:3)

Wonder 251

Since what may be known about God is plain to them, because God has made it plain to them. For since the creation of the world God's invisible qualities—his eternal power and divine nature—have been clearly seen, being understood from what has been made, so that people are without excuse. (Romans 1:19–20)

For he has rescued us from the dominion of darkness and brought us into the kingdom of the Son he loves, in whom we have redemption, the forgiveness of sins. (Colossians 1:13–14)

Immortality 254

And the dust returns to the ground it came from, and the spirit returns to God who gave it. (Ecclesiastes 12:7)

Do not be afraid of those who kill the body but cannot kill the soul. Rather, be afraid of the One who can destroy both soul and body in hell. (Matthew 10:28)

And so we know and rely on the love God has for us. God is love. Whoever lives in love lives in God, and God in them. (1 John 4:16)

The Yearning 257

For now we see only a reflection as in a mirror; then we shall see face to face. Now I know in part; then I shall know fully, even as I am fully known. (1 Corinthians 13:12)

Therefore we do not lose heart. Though outwardly we are wasting away, yet inwardly we are being renewed day by day. For our light and momentary troubles are achieving for us an eternal glory that far outweighs them all. So we fix our eyes not on what is seen, but on what is unseen, since what is seen is temporary, but what is unseen is eternal. (2 Corinthians 4:16–18)

Metaphors of Resurrection 240

Jesus said to her, "I am the resurrection and the life. The one who believes in me will live, even though they die." (John 11:25)

Jesus replied, "The hour has come for the Son of Man to be glorified. Very truly I tell you, unless a kernel of wheat falls to the ground and dies, it remains only a single seed. But if it dies, it produces many seeds. Anyone who loves their life will lose it, while anyone who hates their life in this world will keep it for eternal life." (John 12:23–25)

Afterlife Kisses   243

Have I not commanded you? Be strong and courageous. Do not be afraid; do not be discouraged, for the Lord your God will be with you wherever you go. (Joshua 1:9)

Ask the Lord your God for a sign, whether in the deepest depths or in the highest heights. (Isaiah 7:11)

We are hard pressed on every side, but not crushed; perplexed, but not in despair. (2 Corinthians 4:8)

When the Veil Becomes Thin   246

Very truly I tell you, whoever hears my word and believes him who sent me has eternal life and will not be judged but has crossed over from death to life. (John 5:24)

I write these things to you who believe in the name of the Son of God so that you may know that you have eternal life. This is the confidence we have in approaching God: that if we ask anything according to his will, he hears us. (1 John 5:13–14)

Thoughts on Truth   247

I the Lord do not change. (Malachi 3:6)

Jesus answered, "I am the way and the truth and the life. No one comes to the Father except through me." (John 14:6)

We Are Either Moving Toward God or Away From God   250

Ask and it will be given to you; seek and you will find; knock and the door will be opened to you. For everyone who asks receives; the one who seeks finds; and to the one who knocks, the door will be opened. (Matthew 7:7–8)

Barren Peaks and Lush Valleys   252

The Lord is my strength and my defense; he has become my salvation. He is my God, and I will praise him, my father's God, and I will exalt him. (Exodus 15:2)

It is God who arms me with strength and keeps my way secure. He makes my feet like the feet of a deer; he causes me to stand on the heights. (2 Samuel 22:33–34)

So do not fear, for I am with you; do not be dismayed, for I am your God. I will strengthen you and help you; I will uphold you with my righteous right hand. (Isaiah 41:10)

God Turns Darkness into Light   254

The Lord is my light and my salvation— whom shall I fear? The Lord is the stronghold of my life—of whom shall I be afraid? (Psalm 27:1)

For God, who said, "Let light shine out of darkness," made his light shine in our hearts to give us the light of the knowledge of God's glory displayed in the face of Christ. (2 Corinthians 4:6)

I Meet You, God   258

But may you have mercy on me, Lord; raise me up, that I may repay them. (Psalm 41:10)

Whether you turn to the right or to the left, your ears will hear a voice behind you, saying, "This is the way; walk in it." (Isaiah 30:21)

Humble yourselves, therefore, under God's mighty hand, that he may lift you up in due time. Cast all your anxiety on him because he cares for you. (1 Peter 5:6–7)

Living in the Kingdom   261

Your kingdom is an everlasting kingdom, and your dominion endures through all generations. The Lord is trustworthy in all he promises and faithful in all he does. (Psalm 145:13)

Trust in the Lord with all your heart and lean not on your own understanding; in all your ways submit to him, and he will make your paths straight. (Proverbs 3:5–6)

I Live On   264

Whether you turn to the right or to the left, your ears will hear a voice behind you, saying, "This is the way; walk in it." (Isaiah 30:21)

And we know that in all things God works for the good of those who love him, who have been called according to his purpose. (Romans 8:28)

Thankful   267

Let them give thanks to the Lord for his unfailing love and his wonderful deeds for mankind, for he satisfies the thirsty and fills the hungry with good things. (Psalm 107:8–9)

Give thanks to the Lord, for he is good; his love endures forever. (1 Chronicles 16:34)

Fear Not   270

The Lord is with me; I will not be afraid. What can mere mortals do to me? (Psalm 118:6)

Now the Lord is the Spirit, and where the Spirit of the Lord is, there is freedom. (2 Corinthians 3:17)

When the Impossible Occurs   271

Jesus looked at them and said, "With man this is impossible, but with God all things are possible." (Matthew 19:26)

Everything is possible for one who believes. (Mark 9:23)

Death Falls Into Darkness   276

Since the children have flesh and blood, he too shared in their humanity so that by his death he might break the power of him who holds the power of death—that is, the devil—and free those who all their lives were held in slavery by their fear of death. (Hebrews 2:14–15)

And I heard a loud voice from the throne saying, "Look! God's dwelling place is now among the people, and he will dwell with them. They will be his people, and God himself will be with them and be their God. 'He will wipe every tear from their eyes. There will be no more death' or mourning or crying or pain, for the old order of things has passed away." (Revelation 21:3–5)

Put Your Trust in God   277

Those who know your name trust in you, for you, Lord, have never forsaken those who seek you. (Psalm 9:10)

We demolish arguments and every pretension that sets itself up against the knowledge of God, and we take captive every thought to make it obedient to Christ. (2 Corinthians 10:5)

Heaven   281

He will swallow up death forever. The Sovereign Lord will wipe away the tears from all faces; he will remove the disgrace of his people from all the earth. The Lord has spoken. (Isaiah 25:8)

See, I will create new heavens and a new earth. The former things will not be remembered, nor will they come to mind. (Isaiah 65:17)

He will wipe every tear from their eyes. There will be no more death or mourning or crying or pain, for the old order of things has passed away. (Revelation 21:4)

An Unexamined Faith   282

Believe in the Lord Jesus, and you will be saved—you and your household. (Acts 16:31)

And without faith it is impossible to please God, because anyone who comes to him must believe that he exists and that he rewards those who earnestly seek him. (Hebrews 11:6)

In Closing . . .

I Believe   286

But those who hope in the Lord will renew their strength. They will soar on wings like eagles; they will run and not grow weary, they will walk and not be faint.
(Isaiah 40:31)

Now faith is confidence in what we hope for and assurance about what we do not see.
(Hebrews 11:1)

Author's Note   289

"Because he loves me," says the Lord, "I will rescue him; I will protect him, for he acknowledges my name. He will call on me, and I will answer him; I will be with him in trouble; I will deliver him and honor him."
(Psalm 91:14–15)

The Spirit of the Sovereign Lord is on me, because the Lord has anointed me to proclaim good news to the poor. He has sent me to bind up the brokenhearted, to proclaim freedom for the captives and release from darkness for the prisoners. (Isaiah 61:1)

Then you will know the truth and the truth will set you free. . . . So if the Son sets you free, you will be free indeed. (John 8:32, 36)

ABOUT THE AUTHOR

RHONDA DAWES MILNER IS A RETIRED licensed physician and board certified radiologist. She received her Medical Degree (MD) from Emory University School of Medicine and her residency training in Radiology at the Emory Affiliated Hospitals in Atlanta, GA. She is a summa cum laude and Phi Beta Kappa graduate of the University of Georgia with a BS in microbiology. She is also a graduate of Richmont Graduate University with two master's degrees in professional counseling (2013) and in ministry (2015).

Her counseling specialties are Spirituality & Counseling and Addiction, and her focuses in her practice integrate spirituality with counseling, mindfulness, and grief counseling. Rhonda is a Licensed Professional Counselor (LPC) and a therapist in private practice; counseling is a ministry for her, as she often sees clients who cannot afford regular counseling. She is also a certified spiritual director, and she completed the Renovaré Institute's two-year program in spiritual formation and discipleship (2013), taught by the late Dallas Willard, Gary Moon, James Bryan Smith, Kenneth Boa, and others. (She has been a longtime student of Kenneth Boa's.) In addition, Rhonda is an ordained nondenominational minister. One of her greatest joys is performing the wedding ceremonies of those she loves, as a gift to them.

The mantra she has learned for life is Romans 8:28: "And we know that in all things God works for the good of those who love him, who have been called according to his purpose."

She also founded Healing Presence Ministry, which can be viewed on Facebook, Instagram, and at www.healingpresenceministry.com. Her blog consists of her spiritual writings and poetry.

Rhonda is the mother of four children and has been married for many years. She lost her twenty-five-year-old son in April 2011 to shallow water blackout. She is founder and chairwoman of Shallow Water Blackout Prevention. She has spoken nationally on this topic and been interviewed by Dr. Sanjay Gupta (the interview can be viewed at shallowwaterblackoutprevention.org) and national syndications. She was recognized by Aquatics International in 2012 as one of the Power 25—people changing the aquatics industry. She was also the cofounder of New Leash on Life, a companion-animal advocacy group.

Twenty percent of all profits from the sale of this book will go toward spreading God's love through Healing Presence Ministry, saving lives through Shallow Water Blackout Prevention, opioid addition prevention and treatment, and mental illness awareness and treatment.

Rhonda speaks to groups, giving her testimony about how the power of faith can transform life's worst tragedies. She enjoys reading and sharing her poetry as it allows her heart to sing to others.